See p 124
p 116

Also by the author

Digging Out

Up the Sandbox

Long Division

Torch Song

Generation Without Memory

Your Child's Mind
(with Dr. Herman Roiphe)

Lovingkindness

A SEASON FOR HEALING

REFLECTIONS ON THE HOLOCAUST

Anne Roiphe

SUMMIT BOOKS
NEW YORK LONDON TORONTO SYDNEY TOKYO

Summit Books
Simon & Schuster Building
Rockefeller Center
1230 Avenue of the Americas
New York, New York 10020

Designed by Deirdre C. Amthor

Manufactured in the United States of America

10 9 8 7 6 5 4 3 2 1

Library of Congress Cataloging-in-Publication Data
Roiphe, Anne Richardson
A season for healing : reflections on the Holocaust / Anne Roiphe.
p. cm.
ISBN 0-671-66753-X
1. Holocaust, Jewish (1939–1945)—Influence. 2. Jews—Politics and government—1948– 3. Antisemitism. I. Title.
D804.3.R65 1988 88-21537
940.53′15′03924—dc19 CIP
ISBN 0-671-66753-X

For Rabbi Wolfe Kelman: my friend and teacher

Contents

To My Friends

I have written this book not as a person uniquely qualified in the areas of political science, theology, or history. I am not a survivor or a child of a survivor. I have worked as a journalist, asking questions, reading and reading more. I understand that this is an awesome subject and like an anti-Icarus, this journalist may be flying too close to the dark. But as an American Jew, as a mother who wants her children's children to survive, as a writer, I could not stop thinking about what the events of 1941–1945 meant, what they have become, what we can make of what we know and have experienced. There is anger in the writing of this book, anger from a Jewish point of view and anger from a human point of view. The book is about healing, but this anger would not be kept away, could not be kept out of it, and so I have allowed it to roll through these pages in the hopes that the expression, the openness of feeling, would lead finally to a better place.

This book is part of a long continuous argument, not one that belongs exclusively to the academy or in the yeshiva but the kind that caused families to do battle over the dinner table, one that steamed in editorials in newspapers, Yiddish, German, Czech, Hebrew, French, and English, letters answering the editorials, voices raised, debate that ebbed and flowed across the continent and over the oceans, debate that came with the immigrants along with their memories of mothers and fathers they would never see again.

The argument gains force from the opinions of Socialists who despair of the Anarchists who in turn despise the Zionists who mock the religious ones who point fingers at them, quoting Mishnah and Maimonides in response to Herzl and Marx. The argument continues in Paris and in Mexico City, in Kiev and on the Lower East Side and the Upper West Side and the cafeteria in City College and on the steps of the library of Brooklyn College where the Leninists were fighting with the Trotskyites, and always among them were the Stalinists, grim-lipped, wishing the lot of them bellyaches and incurable coughs. The Rosenbergs are guilty, the Rosenbergs are innocent. The Hitler-Stalin pact is treason, it is rumor. The comrades in Spain have taken to assassinating the Socialists, they have not. The Hellenizers laugh at the ones with Peyot and the ones with covered heads argue with each other, is this more frum or that? What would the Bal Shem have said, and what would the Goan of Vilna have said and what would their grandsons have said? Why did God ask Abraham to sacrifice his only son: why was the forbidden apple planted in the Garden of Eden? Bar Mitzvah boys are planning to engage these questions from the Bimah. Is the Promised Land for man or God to deliver? The Socialists are planning to hold a ball on Yom Kippur. The Zionists want women on tractors and the Tradition wants them behind the curtain and each is sure, absolutely sure, that the truth is in their pocket and the voices go on into the night. This is the people talking and talking, at lunch breaks over machines, at lectures in the evening, at cafés, while picnicking with children. These are the shirtmakers and pants pressers, the boys and girls who study Hebrew and those who play golf on Saturday, the ones who think the future is an illusion and the ones who are logical and the ones who are mystical and the ones who follow Freud and the ones who follow Spinoza and the ones who dream of revolution and the ones who wait for redemption. They raise their voices. Sometimes they are bitter and sometimes they are sad. Sometimes they argue themselves into circles and sometimes the reasoning is true and straight and opens the way for others to follow.

The argument changes its shape with the passing decades but its core remains the same, how can we make sense of our history and what can we do to make the future better? The clamor and the noise we make may not be delicate but from it emerges the lines we follow, the practical, political, psychological, religious expression of our intentions. We argue from pain, we argue with anger, but we hope because we are human.

This book joins that argument.

Introduction

THE SEASON

In 1984 Archbishop Valerian Trifa, former member of the Governing Board of the National Council of Churches, his last appeals exhausted, about to board a plane destined for exile in Portugal, banned forever from the land of freedom, liberty, and the pursuit of happiness, said to the press that had gathered at the terminal gate to catch the last American moments of this dark celebrity, "I am not ashamed of my past at all. The preoccupation about the Holocaust among the Jews will backfire." With this dark warning, he left to bake his clean conscience in the white sun of Cascais.

Preoccupation it is. From the numbing shame, from the peculiar silence, from the mute unwillingness to listen mixed with the inability to speak of the first years after, has come a late release, an erupting volcano of witnessing, of survivors, children of survivors, social scientists and psychologists and clergymen, novelists and poets, TV producers, statesmen, philosophers, historians, ethicists, cardinals and mayors, meeting in conferences, planning museums, teaching courses, publishing memoirs and odes to the righteous Gentiles, funding institutions, gathering libraries that then need new buildings, bringing to trial old men with empty eyes who stare into cameras showing their bald heads, their wrinkled hands, the hollows and sagging skin, each mark of age a triumph over justice, a proof of the lateness in the day for vengeance. Preoccupation it is as Jewish fourth graders in

Dallas prepare the memorial prayers for the dead in Auschwitz, for children like themselves who would now be as old as their grandparents had President Franklin Delano Roosevelt been more compassionate, had America's Jews been less afraid, had our State Department been less old school tie and allowed the ships to dock, had Britain permitted a stay in Palestine, had Vichy France not hurried to comply with orders not yet given.

No one is eager to see a play about the Holocaust. No one longs for another book recording the destruction of another town. We want to forget, to ignore, to go on, and yet we remain preoccupied. We go to the play, we read the book, we watch the movie. The Israeli poet Yehuda Amichai wrote, "Most people in our time have the face of Lot's wife, turned toward the Holocaust, yet always escaping." Preoccupation it is as Orthodox Jews in Brooklyn send wedding invitations to their murdered relatives, addressing the cards to the death camps where they perished. Is it preoccupation or obsession when fifty million dollars' worth of Nazi memorabilia are exchanged each year in a pornographic marketplace where the human imagination can feed on piles of bones stripped of gold teeth and wedding bands?

What does it mean this industry of lecture and writing and museum that is Holocaust, this production of materials that has led to the joke, not a joke, "There's no business like Shoah Business"? Why have the last ten years brought us back with increasing rather than decreasing pressure and intensity to face the events of 1939 to 1945? Many of us believe that in our lifetime the everyday ordinariness of war, famine, oppression, tyranny, was exceeded, something occurred as significant as the Flood, or the gift of fire from Prometheus, or the giving of the tablets at Sinai, or the invention of the wheel, or the discovery of America. Something that makes our moon trips and our laser defense systems seem less wondrous than they might have, something that has changed our view of ourselves and has altered our inner human landscape forever. We have begun to understand that politics and religion will never be the same again. We have each of us to change our conclusions about God, about man, about our safety, about our capacity to hurt others, about the future of our children, our children's children. Our preoccupation, delayed as it was, by the shock waves of trauma, by the slow passage of truth through the body public, is reasonable enough in these unreasonable times. We have lived through a period of history that touches the horizon of myth and forces us to tell the stories over and over, to say nothing, but think everything, or to think too little and say everything. Intellectuals write books about it, publish articles in little periodicals, and rabbis make sermons and pastors make reference and it's on the tip of everyone's tongue, we just don't know quite what to do with it. Like the generation after slavery we are marked by the narrowness of our escape.

Could the archbishop be right? Could this preoccupation with the Holocaust expose the Jewish people to new danger or were those words only the last parry of a skilled orator who in Bucharest in the winter of 1941 spoke so persuasively of the menace of strangers in their midst that his listeners raced through the streets leaving twenty Jewish bodies in the new-fallen snow. Are we the uninvited wedding guest who tells the tale of moral guilt over and over as bells ring and the rest of the party tries to get on with it? Are Jews in the dangerous position of the messenger who carries bad news to the palace? It has different resonances, this matter of the Holocaust, for Jews and non-Jews. What will we make of our preoccupation and what will it make of us?

In *The Days of Simon Stern,* the novelist and theologian Arthur A. Cohen said, "We are obligated to look backward to what has been done. How shall we look forward to what is not yet and with what trust, what hope, what spirit of generativity?"

Several years ago I visited Yad Vashem in the hills outside of Jerusalem. One walks through the corridors surrounded by photographs, cards, short descriptions of entire communities carried off in cattle cars and vaporized in ovens. The halls of the museum are silent even when a crowd is moving slowly on. People do not look at each other as if we were all embarrassed—or is it ashamed? Mourners all, we are in a mausoleum and no one is quite sure of the proper behavior, how to contain the pressure in the chest that increases room to room, what to do with the pounding in the head that grows worse as you emerge into the daylight of a real world accompanied by faces of children about to die. A non-Jewish friend of ours joined us on this visit. Once out into the air we walked past the gardens of the righteous Gentiles, where if you pause for a moment you can catch the heavy scent of wishful thinking as well as the unspoken accusation: if there were righteous Gentiles then the others were less than righteous. Justified or unjustified this reproach hangs over all Holocaust discussion and demands reaction. My friend leaned over to me, noticing my stiffened body and the odd set to my lips. "I can understand," he said sweetly, "why you are so upset." I nodded, he was a friend, after all, who had come to Israel with us out of curiosity. He was a good doctor, a graduate of a New England prep school and Harvard College, a man of honor, a veteran of World War II, where he had served in the infantry, landing in the rough waves and moving damp and frightened over the blood-soaked dunes into Normandy. But why was I upset and he understanding: had we both not had the same experience, seen the same pictures, felt the helplessness of the victim, the mounting power of the technocracy gone wild; had we not both seen the same synagogue in flames? In which case why was it that I was undone and he a sympathetic observer? He understood and I felt? Was the terror I caught from the pictures of the bodies in the ditch, the faces at the barbed wire, the numbers in the explanatory writings, only because I was Jewish and this might have happened to me? Was his understanding, detached and well meaning, because he could never be caught in such a roundup? For my friend the pictures on the wall were of a catastrophe as removed as the Crusades, as the burning of Tyre, as the sacking of Troy, as the marching of Armenians and the burning of witches and the abuses of the Thirty Years' War and the hanging of the Huguenots and the massacres of the Indians across the Arizona bluffs. As a decent civilized man my friend disapproved of all those actions, all those selections, all those examples of the death instinct. For my friend the story of the Holocaust was not unique at all. Not since the birth of Christ have the Jews and the Christians such differing views of an event. This time the sides are reversed and the Christian argues for the historical commonplace and the Jew sees divine interference, because the silence of God is as much a divine event as the birth of God's son: the burning of so many children is surely as significant as the Crucifixion of one son: this time the Jew believes the nature of human understanding is changed forever after. This time the Christian sees only history, humanity, normal life. Ah, what a reversal of roles. This new difference continues and extends the tension between Christian and Jew. For my friend the tour through Yad Vashem produced only the general melancholia that comes when one traces man along his evolutionary path; but for me it was a threat, a specific nightmare, an anger so strong it made of my old friend a mysterious stranger. But my anger also touched my friend. He was on this trip to Israel, after all. He was forced to think about his world and what it could do to others. As a Christian he stood in the same parallel relation to the murderers as I stood to the victims. Neither of us was there but there had come to us. His head was cooler than mine. His point of view was longsighted but his balance too had changed if only slightly. Our friendship had changed.

On the airplane home, as the black-coated, long-bearded men covered in white fringed shawls prayed as the first light of the sun glanced off the metal wings, and babies cried and carts of food moved up and down the aisles, I looked out the window. There suspended in space, the importance of any particular soul was in doubt and I could by an effort of will see Yad Vashem, through my friend's eyes, as just another proof of our expulsion from Eden.

The difference between us was a matter of empathy or sympathy. He was kind but did not feel threatened. I felt enraged. My people are Jews. His are Christians. Mine are Eastern European and his are English from the North Country. Despite shared language, similarity of professions, despite living on the same block for fifteen years, despite being raised in the same corner of America, our tribes are different and this explains a difference in empathy. Would I, touring a museum set up to expose the massacres of the Cambodian peoples by the Khmer Rouge, understand and not feel? Is the limit of empathy at the edge of one's group identity? Why should I feel the death of a Polish Jewish rabbi more deeply than that of an Asian schoolteacher: after all I am neither, have never personally known either. It is this matter of tribal identity that we must explore. We need to look closely at the border where our empathy ends; there our potential for cruelty begins. In the absence of empathy we can hardly imagine the broken bone of someone who is not us, who is other, who is outside. In these years, while the Holocaust is being turned into myth, solidified as history, being used differently by Christian and Jew, we must not cover our mirrors with cloth as if we were in permanent mourning but look, look at our reflections, examine ourselves carefully for the odd growth or the permanent defect.

Immediately in approaching the Holocaust we stumble on multiple paradoxes, one after another, unresolvable contradictions that hold truth in opposites. The first is the question of universality vs. particularity. The difference between my response to Yad Vashem and my Christian friend's contains this argument. One side believes, and on this subject most beliefs are passionate, that the Holocaust was unique, unprecedented, and forever altering the course of human history. The other side maintains that it was part of a continuum, just another example of human evil, of our inability to control the forces of destruction that bide within. Both sides of this discussion are right. Here is the first Holocaust paradox. The second revolves around the argument that after the Holocaust silence is necessary. Lawrence Langer, in his book, *The Holocaust and the Literary Imagination,* reports that the critic T. W. Adorno has proposed that poetry after the Holocaust is barbaric. Silence is the right response to horror beyond comprehension. Language fails and stumbles into absurdity before the crematoria. Art, as it tries to make aesthetic sense, harmony, and unity out of chaos, violates the suffering of the victims, violates our sense of justice. These thoughts are correct. We all recognize them as so and yet the number of words already employed to talk about the Holocaust now require a separate section in the library where the shelves wind on and on.

The other side of the paradox is that we must tell the world what happened. The survivors are bound to witness, to call for justice, to expose the crime, to let the record see every last detail, every moment of the execution of a people. This commandment to witness has been honored even as the evocation of silence has shadowed our novels, poems, histories, and films. Arthur A. Cohen wrote: "We shall do differently than did others in the lineage of our past. We shall not make the world worse that we might be saved, nor shall we make it better that they might be saved. We shall hold up to the world the mirror of its desecration. We shall become the death's-head of the world, the skull through whose eyes and apertures the world will see itself." Yes, but this cannot be done in silence: a paradox.

And here is another. Jews around the world know that the destruction of European Jewry binds them in a shroud of grief and dignity to the Jewish nation. Jewish identity whether we like it or not is reinforced, cemented, locked into place by the six million dead. The theologian philosopher Emil Fackenheim has said that the 614th commandment must be not to hand Hitler a posthumous victory by taking another Jew out of the nation. At the same time the concept of the Chosen People, of a God that protects if you hold up your end of the covenant, has been considerably weakened. Rabbi Richard Rubenstein wrote in *Commentary* magazine, August 1966, "When I say we live in the time of the death of God, I mean that the thread uniting God, and Man, Heaven and Earth has broken. We stand in a cold, silent, unfeeling cosmos, unaided by any purposeful power beyond our own resources. After Auschwitz what else can a Jew say about God?" Jewish identity becomes harder to maintain when the theological historical, national underpinnings have been shaken, if not demolished. So the continuance of the Jewish people is simultaneously reinforced and weakened in the aftershock: another paradox.

Another form of the universal vs. particular paradox is the most unpleasant argument about the identity, the label on the victim's body. Was this a Jewish tragedy or was it a broader tragedy encompassing other groups? The Holocaust was a Jewish catastrophe. This statement is undoubtedly true but it was also a horror for Poles, for Gypsies, and for political dissidents and resistance fighters and peoples of all sorts who suffered hunger and loss under the Nazi assault. This too is true. To erase the uniquely Jewish nature of the tragedy is to deny the intent of the Nazis to destroy all Jews. To deny the intent of the Nazis is to violate the memory of the dead by merging their unique identity in an inchoate human mass. But to ignore the non-Jewish victims is to deny their reality and their dignity and to continue to shore up the fences that divide people instead of emphasizing the common humanity of all the victims. To ignore the deaths of non-Jews leads us to cooperate with the Nazi turn of mind because we are talking about that very same common humanity that was vigorously denied by those who gathered at the Wannsee Conference and planned the Final Solution: to make Jewish death different from other death is to build higher the wall between Jewish life and other life, an impossible position: a paradox.

Israel, a political state, a state like any other, was born out of the ashes of the camps. The nations of the world had a second of pity, a moment of horror, and they made a state for the survivors so that the genocide could not be repeated, would happen never again. But by gathering so many Jews in one place, a place surrounded by eighty million enemies, by causing another group to enter a diaspora, the Jews are threatened; a mass murder of Jews, if it happens again, is most likely to happen in the state and because of the state that had been created to avoid such catastrophe: an irony if not a paradox. In Israel the Jews are now occupiers, creators of second-class citizenship, fearful of a group living within its midst, angry with people of another religion, of another group. The Israelis are not Germans nor have they behaved in any way like Nazis, but the ironies are there, the echo is there, the situation is set up for a replay of events, certainly the resonances are exploited by enemies of Israel.

As the effects of the Holocaust unfold, as we explore the political, religious, and psychological problems that followed the survivors to America and to Israel, we will see these paradoxes and ironies again and again pulling us in different directions, festering in surprising ways.

The forty years since the end of World War II have not healed the wound. It is still an open question whether or not the Holocaust marks the end of the Jewish experience as it has been for centuries or is just another in the cycles of temples destroyed, walls built and breached, diaspora, exile, and return. While we will not remain as focused as we are today on the Holocaust, for the generations to come it will remain a central historical and religious event. We will not be able to feel about it as intensely as we do now. Time is on the side of erosion of feeling. This present state of affairs where each week *The New York Times* publishes at least one or two articles and letters dealing with Holocaust events, where publishers swim in survivors' memoirs, and fund-raising letters for memorials and museums arrive with each batch of mail cannot last. Soon there will be a surfeit.

Soon the survivors' voices will fade and the last of the war criminals will have been placed behind glass and executed, or died of old age. The next generation will be free of responsibility and free to mythologize and theologize without the check of reality. They will make something else out of this human disaster and they will build on what we have said, and what we have concluded, and so it is especially important now that we examine the way in which we use and understand the history of the war against the Jews.

We must also be scrupulous in examining our emotional condition. We know that a sense of helplessness, a great fear, a powerful but unreleased, unrecognized rage is dangerous for an individual mind, so also it can harm the communal life, affecting it in subterranean ways, driving it to positions not entirely reasonable, not always prepared to improve matters. Here is Sonja Milner, a survivor, eighteen years old when the war ended, who writes in her memoir, with unusual candor of feelings that most of us have learned to repress, to deny. She writes that she was liberated from Auschwitz and was traveling with a friend among the last flares of war. "One day we experienced a sense of deep satisfaction. As we were walking about in the city we saw some Germans lying in the fields. Those Germans had fled Danzig and were staying in the fields with their wives and children. A battalion of Russian Soldiers passed by. The soldiers fell upon the Germans and began to rape the young girls, the women and the children. Some ten or twenty fell upon a little girl and raped her. We watched and beamed with satisfaction. We were finally being avenged. For a Jew cannot avenge himself. We once thought that if we came out alive we would take vengeance but how could a Jew take revenge? We were sick and weak and hungry. But now we saw how the Russian Soldiers had wrought vengeance upon them: how they had torn them to pieces, those Germans in the fields. We were entitled to that satisfaction. It was a legitimate reaction, a natural all-too-human response on our part. At that scene of rape and violence, another picture superimposed itself. It was my own nieces and nephews that I saw being ripped apart by the Germans. My nieces and nephews were seven, five, and three years old. Still our revenge was vicarious."

Jews have stated that they are not seeking revenge in a literal sense. They have declared officially that they are not looking for a position of moral superiority or moral excuse. But these statements while intellectually honest and real and come from a long rabbinical ethical tradition which has consistently emphasized reconciliation and forgiveness, still cannot undo the normal, human emotional feelings that some Jews do have and that affect our considerations about the Holocaust and the world around us.

And so as Jews our shared rage, rage now at least two generations old, our frustrated desire for vengeance, our fearfulness, affect our political positions and will shape our actions, our moral choices, our designs for living in the years to come. That Jews are angry is a fact. That this anger makes others uneasy is also a fact. Everyone wants to be good, to belong to a good group and a good nation. The need to believe oneself morally good seems to motivate human behavior almost as strongly as the need for love and sex. When Jews insist on recalling the Holocaust, when Jews express their anger and their pain about the Holocaust, then they are directly or indirectly accusing others of not being good and these implicit or explicit accusations cause terrible anger. When people feel guilty they feel vastly uncomfortable and then they become angry with the group or person who has made them feel guilty. In the last forty years the Jews have made many people feel guilty and many people angry. Now collective responsibility and collective guilt, especially passed on from one generation to another, are quite obviously unacceptable and unnecessary. But guilt for something one's nation or one's religious group did or did not do apparently can light up the most difficult of passions. As we examine the effects of the Holocaust we come directly into the angers felt by all sides. If we are going to move on, we have to allow and respect those feelings, hard as they are for us, much as we might wish Sonja Milner had wept for the German girls raped in their fields.

How we balance the paradoxes built into our considerations of the Holocaust, how Christians and Jews learn to live with the past, how we turn the raw material into myth and history and moral lesson, may bring us to what matters and what does not. This book will probe the repercussions of the Holocaust on the past and present connections between Jews and Catholics, Jews and Poles, Jews and blacks, Israel and the world, Jews and the USSR. It will examine how the trauma of the Holocaust and the Christian response reverberate today in our literature and in our thoughts. Sometimes this book will be angry and difficult because the feelings aroused can only be tamed if we are willing to look at them, to live with them awhile, to see them at work among us.

Some have said that the Holocaust was a miniature nuclear war. It was a warning to mankind of what we can do to each other. It has been said that the Jews of World War II served like the canaries placed in small cages on miners' caps. If the canary dies, the miner knows that fatal gas is leaking into the mine. Well, the Jews did die and our mines are very dangerous places. If we cannot learn to live in tribes without tribal warfare (and what are nations if not tribes writ large), we will not, with the technology at our disposal, survive. If Jew and non-Jew may come to new understanding, we may explore ways to prevent future acts of unthinkable, now thinkable destruction. This book talks about the catastrophe of the past and how its paradoxes have marked us, because most of us no longer believe that history is a story without an end. Before we can heal we must find a way to face Medusa without mirrors, to accept how angry, guilty, distressed Jew and Gentile still feel. Perhaps then we can have a change of seasons.

Christians and Jews

TWO TESTAMENTS—ONE HISTORY

When I was traveling through the Midwest in 1983 talking on TV and radio call-in shows about a book on Jewish identity, I received at least twenty on-air calls from irate listeners who said one after another, with different degrees of politeness, "What is this endless talk about the Holocaust. I'm tired of it. I didn't do anything to anyone. I wish the Jews would stop trying to make me feel guilty." I heard also the logical next step from at least one radio-show host, one TV interviewer, and several call-ins: "I don't believe it ever happened at all. Historians say that the Jews just made it up to get pity, to get the Arab land." Some historians are indeed saying just that.

In Germany in June 1986 Edward Nolte, the historian, wrote a piece in the conservative newspaper *Frankfurter Allgemeine Zeitung*. Despite the fact that his article was titled "A Past That Would Not Disappear," his point was that the atrocities of wartime Germany were nothing compared to the atrocities of Stalin's Gulag and that Hitler and his generals were simply doing their best to win the war against the East. The camps were patterned after Stalin's design and were intended to resist the Asian peril. This argument does not explain why Hitler needed to exterminate millions of Jewish families in order to protect Germany from Stalin, but it does serve to blur the distinctions between horrors and to place Germany in a less blameworthy position, leaving the responsibility on the shoulders of the despised and feared Russians. The intent of this thinking is to ease German conscience while passing the guilt eastward. It places the aggression of the Nazis in the context of a Cold War prologue and makes Germany, America's ally all along: trompe l'oeil history or Hitler and Houdini as the opening bill at the Paramount. Nolte's article has been seriously discussed in newspapers, in periodicals all over Germany. As cowardly, self-serving, conscience-relieving, pride-enhancing a maneuver as this may be, it is nevertheless a solution to an obviously intolerable burden of guilt. To deny or distort the reality of the Holocaust provides balm for the still open wounds of collective national pride.

Jacques Vergès, the defense counsel for Klaus Barbie, head of the Gestapo at Lyons, France, argues that his client is innocent because other atrocities, comparable atrocities, went unpunished, such as those at My Lai, in French Algeria, in the Arab village of Deir Yassin in 1948. To equate all massacres with the Holocaust, to blend the varieties of human violence into one violence, is to take the focus off the Jews and their persecutors. It seems odd to argue that because other murderers have gone free the one at hand deserves release. But the argument is carefully designed to reduce the Jewish moral position, to wash the Jews with the blood that is on others' hands. Author, Nobel Prize winner, Elie Wiesel testified at the trial and said to reporters, about Mr. Vergès, who is known in France as an advocate of the Arab position, "He was full of hatred, hatred for me personally, hatred for the Jewish people and hatred for the victims." Certainly Vergès has a desperate argument and one that tells us how painful, how enraging it must be to live today with the guilt of the camps and see a Jew, a former pariah whose life was once worth only the price of his hair and his dentistry, now receiving a Nobel Prize for telling the world what occurred during the Third Reich. Since the early 1970s, anti-Semitic historians have been circulating theories that the Holocaust is a Jewish Zionist invention intended to create false sympathy for the Jews, and this absurd fiction has surfaced in Canada and Japan as well as in the universities of France and Spain. Removing the death camps from the center of the historical stage fits very nicely into political agendas. It suits those who have long believed in Zionist conspiracies, and while the circulation and acceptance of such a cruel reversal of truth seems incredible, an affront to sanity as well as morality, we have to recognize that this is the tip of the iceberg, the radical version of the "stop making me feel guilty, I didn't do it," response that must be deeply rooted in Western society. On May 31, 1987, a community of survivors in Skokie, Illinois, dedicated a Holocaust memorial, a bronze statue. The next morning before dawn, swastikas defaced the monument and the word "Liar" was written in large letters across the base of the sculpture. Not even for twenty-four hours could the guilt be endured. An angry cry, a graffiti protest, an expression of hate, yes; but also a complaint against the inherent accusation that seemed to come from the statue, from the dedication, from the presence among the living of the once declared dead.

The cry of denial tells us that the Jewish witness, the Jewish call for revenge, for atonement, for understanding, falls not on neutral ears, not into the hearts of rescuers and innocents but onto much of European civilization, all implicated in a breakdown of morality, a breakthrough of sadistic force, all implicated either through action or omission of action, implicated because the culture itself bred the climate that permitted the barbarism, because the safety catches, the civilizing forces of Church and art and education all proved useless against the storm.

That righteous Gentiles appeared in almost all countries and rescued Jews, joined the resistance, and risked their own lives and the lives of their families does not undercut the basic fact that all, Jew and Christian alike, know. The world itself, civilization, its governments, its churches, its doctors, its farmers, and businessmen looked the other way, did not interfere effectively or in time or with enough commitment to stop the slaughter. We tell each other anecdotes of little villages where Jewish children were protected, of whole families saved by generous and courageous souls, but we tell those tales like fairy stories, meant to make promises that cannot be kept. We need those stories because they, like beautiful gold door knockers on the house of prostitution, make it possible to believe in the work of civilization just as you are about to open the door to bestiality. The facts of the Holocaust threaten not only German pride and nationalism but all of Christendom's self-image. The SS were referred to by other Germans as pastors' sons. The combination of Nietzsche and Vulcan may have produced comic-opera politics with tragic results, but the failure to stay their hand is Christian, Christian Sunday schools, Christian academies, Christian boys brought up reading the Gospels in chapel at Eton and Yale, taught the things that Calvin wanted them to know, repeating the anti-Semitic libels of Martin Luther, listening to the sermons of the pope: they made the decisions not to bomb train tracks, not to permit refugees over closed borders. They made the decision to turn away when the roundups occurred in their towns. They demonstrated clearly that Christian society for the most part turns the other cheek to allow a more pleasant view.

Christians have responded in various ways to make sense of the events and to preserve their faith in their religious and moral structures. Walter Burkhardt, professor of theology at the Catholic University of America, has turned the entire Jewish people into a form of Christ. He calls the Jews, "a people that has survived every persecution and borne ceaseless witness to the suffering servant of Yahweh. God is here, and He speaks to and through the Jew, His suffering servant." This language is like New York's John Cardinal O'Connor's, who in trying to make sense of the Holocaust speaks of the, "mysteries of suffering." Our religious imaginations have always dwelled on pain and blood as a means to bring us closer to God. The word Holocaust means burnt offering and the idea of a communal sacrifice to purify the others, to purge evil, and to win God's favor is an ancient idea. It follows from the Flood and the destruction of Sodom and Gomorrah. It is an extension of our primitive sacrifices of animals and hostages to thirsty gods who created the weather or were the weather as the case may be. Sacrificing sons is also an ancient and venerable tradition; from Abraham to God Himself there has been the temptation to cause the favored, most beloved children fright, pain, and fear of abandonment. But when one speaks of the offering of six million, the sacrifice for purification purposes of whole communities left heaving in the ditches, then the poetry in the idea disappears. Nevertheless the Christian need to give religious meaning to Jewish suffering is understandable. For Jews the dilemma is compounded. They must solve the paradox of a Chosen People apparently chosen to suffer more than any other. Jewish history is a long line of disaster and recovery and could possibly accommodate one more swing of the cycle from destruction to redemption, but the repetitions can no longer be as comforting as they once were, and the matter of chosenness becomes increasingly more of a scourge than a gift. If meaning cannot be found for the Jews' election as God's People other than to be the scapegoat for the nations, the sacrificial offering of the high priests of other religions, a people for whom there is no ram in the thicket, then the world increases in senselessness, in emptiness, in moral vacuity, and the tenets of all religions are threatened.

The Reverend Jimmy Swaggart, who has himself dabbled in sin, said to his TV audience that, "the reason there has been so little peace in the Mideast is because Israel as a people turned its back on the God of Abraham, Isaac, and Jacob and embraced pagan idols." Jews have yielded, he said, "too often to philosophies that have been harmful to mankind; such as Marx, Freud, Trotsky and Dewey." He learned this from the Jewish Bible. He is using ancient Jewish self-accusations to distance himself from the Wandering Jew whose ideas have become an irritant to proper Christian order. If one can blame the victim, guilt is drained away as if by magic, thank the Lord. The same Reverend Swaggart showed his twenty-million audience a documentary film of the concentration camps, and in a voice over the pictures of emaciated men and women standing at the barbed-wire fence, over the camera panning through the barracks and on the dead bodies piled on bunks, the Reverend Swaggart explained to his audience that this had happened to the Jews because they had not accepted Jesus Christ. Well, we can all agree he has a powerful object lesson there. His conclusions spared Christianity from moral responsibility for the disaster and made sense and order out of a terrifying event that threatens precisely our need for meaning and order. But this tap dance on the graves could only play in the Fundamentalist mind where certainties are the daily bread one is thankful for and reason a toxic substance that has been carted out of town and dumped elsewhere. Some fundamentalist Jews have convinced themselves that the Holocaust was a result of the impiety and impurity of the Jews of Europe. This too seems a violation of graves and reason.

An Austrian half-Jew, Jean Amery, a survivor of Auschwitz, a literary critic, who spent years talking on radio shows throughout Germany, telling people what had happened there, received a letter from a young German telling him that he "was sick and tired of hearing about it." But Jean Amery was not sick and tired of talking about it. He said he wanted the German nation to atone by seeing and admitting the degradation and special horror of the Nazi regime. He wanted everyone to know of the sign he had seen beneath a crèche in Austria, Christmas, 1938: it read, "Let the hungry be fed and the poor be welcome and the Jews shall die like dogs." Amery wanted an admission of guilt. He felt resentment at the economic miracle and he feared that "everything will be submerged in a general century of barbarism." This tug between Christian and Jew, one seeking to submerge the particulars of the event, to make the victim universal, at fault himself, so faceless as to be pitied only in abstraction, like the dead under the ashes of Pompeii, and the other seeking to remember everything, to bring it up again and again, to follow presidents to graveyards and point fingers at dead soldiers, to seek its causes, to describe its techniques, to name its victims, gives guilt to the Christian. It enrages the Jew further as the guilt is denied and pushed away, and the Jew, morally righteous, but isolated, talking to himself, threatening the universe, still carrying around his dead that no one will accept, becomes, in his indignation, a reproach to everyone else.

"There, there on your forehead is a mark, Cain," Jews say, and Cain who hoped it was a small mark, one that could go unnoticed, feels like killing all over again. Jean Amery, weary with his role in this world, was a suicide at age sixty-seven in Zurich.

Anti-Semitism isolated the Jew in Europe. In the final analysis even the assimilated Jew, the war veteran, the cardiologist, the pianist, were all considered part of the disease of Judaism and were removed with the rest. In a sense all modern history was a prelude to the Holocaust, but after the destruction, the surviving Jew remains the one who has not accepted Jesus Christ as true Messiah, a position that created vulnerability before. Now to make him an even less welcome member of Western society, he is also the messenger of the breakdown of religion, the corruption of the state and the Church. Such a witness, such a reproving, unrelentingly accusing moral voice cannot fit easily into the modern world. Anti-Semitism did not die in the crematoria although it was muted, abashed, perhaps even stunned for a while at what it had wrought. But as the years wore on and it became apparent that the Jews had not all vanished and that now they not only rejected Jesus, but they stood with their rejection on high moral ground. They were the only religious group prior to 1945 who, since the birth of Jesus Christ, had not bloodied the earth. Anti-Semitism has again taken on new life, as it denies the meaning and the reality of the Holocaust and as it appears as anti-Zionism, opposition to Israel's right to exist as a state.

In their rejection of what the Christian world believed to be the true Messiah, the Jews have always said they were the Chosen People, they had a special Covenant and a religion worth dying for, and this position, which probably infuriated pagans across the ancient world, is now compounded by the Christian failure, by the simple facts of Jewish death. Jews have attempted to explain this matter of chosenness to the Christian world and mitigate its sting. They have claimed that they have a mission, obligation, not a special or favored place among the peoples of the earth. They have said that they are simply doing what God has asked of them, separate but not superior or better loved. However, the insistence of the Jews since Hellenic times on being a people apart, a people who dwell alone, a people who cannot eat the food of other peoples, who follow a different set of fast days, feast days, and who try to keep their children within the fold, has not convinced the world that Jews consider themselves merely different and not indeed better. The truth, despite the diplomatic words of our more political rabbis, is that Jews do feel that they have been elected, have been willing to die to protect that election; they have been told for millennia that they are inferior but in their hearts they have believed that they are superior. This is not the official Jewish position but it is the all-too-human belief of a people whose sense of self-worth has been often attacked and who needed a defense, a way of viewing themselves that would preserve their pride. The human way is to set up ranks and place oneself at the head. Jews, like everyone else, have done this too. The Diaspora Jew has believed that while he is superior in being Jewish he is also inferior in being Jewish. The capacity to hold both contradictory positions at once is part of the ambiguity, the humor, the wit, the madness of the modern Jew. The Holocaust, even while causing profound damage to Jewish pride and dignity, reinforced the sense of moral victory. That was the only part of the Jew that could not be burned or buried. The victims lost everything but their moral position.

•

Just on the other side of Jewish righteousness is Jewish humiliation. The many years that passed before most Jews were able to talk clearly about the Holocaust reveal not only shock but also shame. The survivors getting off boats and arriving in their American relatives' homes were greeted with injunctions not to talk about the past; at first, hard as it is to believe today, no one wanted to hear details. It was bad enough to know the vague outline and disastrous result. Shame and humiliation are most uncomfortable feelings and even young Israelis react in this way. During the trial in 1987 of John Demjanjuk, accused of being Ivan the Terrible, the Treblinka guard, Ehud Offer, a thirty-two-year-old Sabra whose parents came from Romania, wrote to a Tel Aviv newspaper: "It makes me sick. It's humiliating. I just can't believe that 6 million Jews could let such a thing happen to themselves and I don't want to watch a trial that recounts it." This sense of shame, accompanied by a desire to keep the details quiet, is not as unreasonable as it might appear. The Freudian psychoanalyst Kurt Eissler said, in a paper in the *American Journal of Psychiatry,* 1967, "with few exceptions the feeling of contempt for suffering is something of a universal reaction very much alive in all of us." This despite our religious fascination with "the mysteries of suffering," which may well be some attempt to civilize our opposite, more primitive, and probably stronger impulse: to despise the wounded, and to further victimize the victim.

The question of resistance, how much, when, and what kind? the other side of the coin, the question of cooperation, was it necessary, did it go too far? haunts the Jewish mind because we are afraid of the contempt we might feel for ourselves: because we are afraid of the contempt of others. The universal Jewish reaction of glorious joy on the victorious Six-Day War, on the storming of Entebbe, tells us how much we need to erase the image of long lines waiting for death, of faces peering from behind the cracks in cattle cars. It seems a superficial matter, this question of pride, this fear of contempt, after all the death and horror, but the fact remains that we feel it, we feel it acutely. We lost our communal virility along with our illusions of safety among strangers.

Our moral position, our justified rage, produces a certain amount of clear reaction in the Christian world. In 1981, a woman in Chicago called into a radio talk-show program on Jewish identity and said, "I'm tired of being made to feel guilty about the Holocaust. What do the Jews want from me? Good Christians didn't do it. Why can't they just forget it." This reaction is honest. Less honest is the attempt by certain madmen, scholars, teachers, anti-Semites, to deny the events entirely, calling them rumors, Zionist plots to create unwarranted sympathy for the Jews. It is almost as if the Western world has now become a haunted house, and the conscience of the people leads them to fear the retaliation of the murdered, of the restless spirits who hover over the present with the crimes of yesterday unsettled. It is almost as if they could read Sonja Milner's mind as she stood at the side of the field watching the Soviet soldiers rape a little girl, a little girl just as she had been when the Nazis entered her shtetl.

To witness the Holocaust, to anchor it in the center of human experience, was accomplished despite the strong feeling in the immediate aftermath that words themselves were obscene, that language itself had been debased in the camps and that speech was offensive to the dead. The initial response of survivor and nonsurvivor was to mourn in silence, to mourn without style or phrase or grace. The poets who needed to speak also needed not to speak, and the poems were bare, sparse, like fragments found after a fire, turned tightly into themselves. This silence, this attempt at silence in which the voices of the living could echo, could find their own shape and disappear without further human intervention, still surrounds the best of the Holocaust writing, the writing that has become art. Because despite the need for silence, the other need, a human urge: to speak, to accuse, to demand attention, to leave a trace, to understand the ununderstandable, has prevailed. In all of the well-written, true books about the Holocaust that go beyond the reporting of a singular experience, we feel the reluctance of the writer, the hand held over the mouth, the guilt at speaking of the unspeakable, even as the words are coming out. This lends a common mood, a common shape to the best Holocaust literature, binding it together, as it should be, in one volume, too large perhaps for one volume, but one volume nevertheless.

An Israeli writer, Aharon Appelfeld, elegantly builds for us a dream landscape, a Europe of such a nightmare that we move through it half asleep, drugged but amazed that such beauty of language can arise from the terror of human evil. He wants to warn us about assimilation, about trusting, about cultures that appear benign, about the genteel masks murderers wear. He has an agenda that ties his language into the text of Holocaust writing, and while it is art, it is also a sermon. He catches for us the unreality, where nothing is what it appears and time is not a friend and death is advancing with the changing season, a landscape of dislocation that began in those times but lasts into ours. But then all of the Holocaust writers do that, the good and the indifferent ones. When writing on the Holocaust the Jewish artists of various schools and countries are closer to each other, because of the voice that comes out as if reluctant to speak, because of the anger held in check, because of the grief that is a kind of baseline in this writing, because of the nature of their subject, than the artists of any other epoch or nation or grouping.

Aharon Appelfeld's slim books are oblique to the events themselves, but not so oblique that we do not hear them, feel them, know them, to create the brutality of the forest, the cruelty of the peasant, the waves of wandering souls, the obtuseness of the victim who denied. Denial becomes an actor on Appelfeld's stage and death becomes the prompter hiding behind the curtain. Aharon Appelfeld has said that the Holocaust is the metaphor for our century, and he has, waiting for thirty years for it to come clear in his mind, found a way to make the metaphor, still reeking with silence, tell us what we need to know. In the way that ordinary man is not supposed to be able to enter the inner sanctum of the Temple without being destroyed, so it is that we are not supposed to speak of the horror of the Holocaust without violating someone or something. We are supposed to close our mouths in awe the same way we are supposed to close our eyes before the face of God. But some of our writers are true high priests and have brought us into the presence of the terror.

If the Holocaust is the metaphor for our century then it is natural enough that other writers, non-Jewish writers, nonsurvivor writers will also use the material. A metaphor for a century cannot be cordoned off for the use of the victim group alone. Most writers consider themselves high priests and naturally seek the center of the temple, no matter whose name may be over the door of that temple.

However, in this century the subject of the Holocaust is still so fraught with implications of guilt and accusations against ancient and honored belief systems, and there were so few completely innocent bystanders in the Western world, that the initial literature of the Holocaust by Gentiles has been marred by a variety of axes to grind. Holocaust literature by non-Jews does not suffer from the need to keep the silence. It does not radiate the same heat of anger and fear. It seems motivated in part by a desire to universalize the experience: to deny the special Jewish aspect of the tragedy and claim it for all mankind. The argument about the particularity of the Jewish experience and the universality of the Holocaust is entered by English-speaking Christian writers who have chosen this subject. John Hersey's *The Wall,* written closer in time to the event before the accusations and implications surfaced into the general culture, may be the exception that proves the rule. Holocaust writing by Christians in the last ten years seems to answer that argument in ways that will ease Christian guilt in the face of Jewish accusation.

D. M. Thomas's *The White Hotel* attacks both Freud and the Jewish specificity of the Holocaust. He makes his character who appears to be suffering from a hysterical symptom actually a visionary who is foreseeing her own personal tragedy and the historical tragedy that is coming in the future. He then takes the Holocaust and undoes it by uniting all loved ones in a blissful, painless condition in a White Hotel in the Sky. God in fact had a purpose in this destruction, and the vision of a kind of preheaven, a passing-through stage of the human soul after death, is a Christian version of events. The actual suffering is wiped out in the wash of pleasant aftereffects. In *The White Hotel,* a book filled with traditional Christian imagery, from births in mangers to blood sacrifices, the world does make sense and the Deity, while mysterious in His ways, is still guarding us all and creating for us happy endings, ever afters, and religious truths. The Christian writer needs to remove the tragedy from the Jews, to make it part of his own cosmology, his own spirituality. It is natural that non-Jewish writers will handle the subject in their own terms, not so intimate, not so Jewish, but justifying either their religion, their morality, or their version of social meaning. One can read *The White Hotel* as a reclaiming of suffering for the Christian soul and a replacing of the Jewish tragedy and its moral indictment with an erotic, amusing, divine order that wipes out guilt even as it admits Jews into its heaven, into God's scheme of things.

In the issue of June 29, 1978, of *The New York Review of Books,* William Styron wrote an essay called "Hell Reconsidered." While complaining about a TV film on the Holocaust he says, "But despite an offhand allusion to I. G. Farben which seemed both strained and obvious, and a brief reference to the Poles which in the context in which it was made, gave a mistaken impression that theirs was an infinitely more pleasant lot than that of the Jews there was conveyed no sense whatever of the magnitude and deadliness of the slave enterprise. There was no suggestion that in this inconceivable vast encampment of total domination (predominantly Gentile at any given time) were thousands of Poles and Russians and Czechs and Slovenes dying their predetermined and natural deaths, that in droves Catholic priests and nuns were being subjected to excruciating and fatal medical experiments, that members of Polish and other European resistance groups (whose struggle and great courage were never once hinted at in the program) were being tortured and in some cases gassed like the Jews. In short the suffering and martyrdom of these others were ignored to the great loss of historical accuracy and I am afraid of moral responsibility. We shall perhaps never even begin to understand the Holocaust until we are able to discern the shadows of the enormity looming beyond the enormity we already know." Here we have an eloquent plea for the universalism of the Holocaust. But the facts are blurred. The Polish prisoner did indeed fare better than his Jewish counterpart. The slave factories were predominantly Gentile at times only because the Jews had been killed on arrival. Droves of Catholic priests in the ovens is an exaggeration and the fact remains that Europeans who were caught in the Nazi killing machine did have some choice. They had for the most part ways of surviving that were not available to Jews. This makes the experience different for these different groups. Death is death, and horror is horror, but William Styron is in an awful hurry to deny the essence of what happened—which was specifically targeted genocide, one tribe against another. If we do not understand the virus of anti-Semitism, its centrality to the Holocaust, then distortions will abound and we will soon sink into total confusion.

It is not difficult to imagine why William Styron needs to blur the essential Jewish nature of the Holocaust. As a white Christian southerner, he feels uncomfortable about the behavior of his kind toward others. If he shifts the victim to the universal human being, he finds a category in which he himself belongs.

William Styron's *Sophie's Choice* is a book in which the heroine is Polish, the mad villain is Jewish, the hero is a southern Gentile who is the sanest and most humane of all. The hero is the victim both of teasing Jewish princesses and of the vulgarity of Jewish doctors. Styron appears to say that the Holocaust was a human tragedy and not a Jewish one. His book testifies that Christian boys could have a better conscience, a finer intellect, a better sense of values than Jewish ones. By avoiding the good Jews and heralding the good Christian, he helps Gentile readers avoid guilt. He describes a Holocaust that belongs to him, as an innocent, not as a member of the oppressing group. He makes the point that his character Stingo's fine southern father, whose grandfather had owned slaves, was the kindest man alive. He is not tainted by the slavery that brought him wealth and position in the community. Indeed the sins of the fathers should not be heaped on the heads of the children. But because Styron has his own agenda in writing this book, he can tell us the story of Stingo's search for sexual release with the same intensity as Sophie's terrible camp experience. His sense of proportion is vulgar because the material is not inside him or available to him. Styron has a reason for creating Sophie as a Pole and in doing so he pleased many of his readers who also wanted to feel identified with the victims of the tragedy, who are wearied by Jewish accusations, an accusation that comes as any Jew lives, marries, and reproduces, after Hitler. Styron has many readers who also needed to be declared innocent. Styron is not tainted by the cruelties of others. He needs to make the Holocaust a universal, non-Jewish tragedy, in order to undercut the Jewish moral position, in order to make himself equal, a member in good standing in the matter of human suffering. Why is he worrying about this? Why is he protesting so much? Because he is tainted as is the Christian world. Of course this taint is not real guilt for a real action, this taint is the smudge of failure of the Christian endeavor, of the structures of civilization to control the barbarism within. The guilt that Christians may experience makes no objective sense and yet even more stubbornly it is there. If for centuries masses of people believed in the guilt of the Jews for the death of Jesus, then we know that these same masses can feel the genocide of the Jews as a mark against their collective soul. This creates resentment. Jews must listen to this resentment. It could be dangerous at some time. It gives heat to the universal vs. particular argument and it shows us that perhaps this is a disagreement that if we win will only create further divisions between us, divisions that could harm one day. Styron's point is well taken; the slave endeavor, which has afflicted this entire century, is about dominance and unleashed power far more than it is about Jews and Aryans. We will have to find a balance, one that does not erase the Jewish tragedy but gradually enlarges it, so that the world will stop pushing away the Holocaust and can hear its warnings.

Anne Frank's diary is the Holocaust book both Jews and Christians have taken to heart. It is affecting beyond doubt to listen to this young girl struggle with the ordinary pangs of her age while we know the Nazis are closing in and her death is imminent. The quote from Anne Frank that many families have included in their seder readings—"It's really a wonder I haven't dropped all my ideals, because they seem so absurd and impossible to carry out. Yet I keep them, because in spite of everything, I still believe that people are really good at heart"—explains why the whole world, Jewish and non-Jewish, has made Anne Frank the symbol of the catastrophe. The house in which the Frank family was hidden has become a virtual shrine. Many thousands of visitors climb the stairs each year to view pages of the actual diary, to look at photographs and remember. Anne Frank's diary has become so popular because Anne Frank embodies both the horror of the event and the hope of mankind. Her quote tells all of us that this was an error, a slip, a mistake, that really our world is good, we are good. This is something we all can tell our children. We want to believe that at bottom, at heart, in reality, there is goodness out there. Of course what happened to Anne Frank several months after she professed her faith in humankind tells us just the opposite of what this young vulnerable teenager believed. Sentimentality makes us select Anne Frank as our Holocaust martyr and use her quote on the goodness of human nature in our liturgy.

We all know better. The correct quote would read, "Because of everything, I no longer will depend on the goodness of people." But the popular, most accepted Holocaust literature has been the most hopeful, the most optimistic about the future and gives the reader, after a good cry, a chance to step forward renewed. This is not art or truth, but it is popular culture which is always busy putting a face on things, helping us to muddle through.

The mass affection for Anne Frank as a symbol of the Nazi cruelty and human hope almost equals the world's love of Saint Joan. Richard Gilman, professor of drama at Yale University, says that, "We have more books, plays, movies, about St. Joan than any other figure in History with the exception of Jesus Christ." But Saint Joan was a fighter, a brilliant military strategist, and her death at the stake came only after she had indeed saved France. In the years 1941–1945 the Jews had many fighters. They died in forests and in battle, but their stories, although available, have not caught the imagination of the world in the way that Anne Frank's has, a young girl whose diaries are most remarkable in their ordinary details, for the commonness of the life she longed for and the goodness she believed would save her. Why has a young female come to represent the lost six million? Perhaps because by focusing on her, Jew and Christian can avoid certain painful questions. The Jewish male was unmanned. He could not defend his children or his wife. His humiliation is perhaps covered over by the choice of a young nonthreatening girl to represent the Holocaust. It is easy to understand that the Christian mind would particularly appreciate a young girl who has expressed the sentiment that the world is not guilty of incurable evil. It is easier to like her than some male who might be seen as angry, threatening, or be tarred with the anti-Semitic canards that hang in the air along with the other irrepressible viruses. The Christian needs to be told he is good, the Jew needs to believe it. Anne Frank suits everyone. But from the point of view of Jewish pride, from the point of view of Jewish survival, how much better it would have been if she had been given a chance to lead into battle. If voices had told her to obtain a gun and kill a Gestapo agent from her attic window. Saint Joan is about the world of politics and men as they really are. Anne Frank is our way of not facing what we know.

Hannah Senesch, who has become something of a figure in Israel, was a fighter but she failed her mission. She too was a writer of diaries and hers contain grandiose, adolescent fantasies of greatness. The sound of her ego as it scratches its way across the pages is painful, especially against the background of the tragedy in which so many private human expectations were so soon to be aborted. Why has she become a known persona? Here we have another young girl and one whose life was saved because she had left for Palestine before it was too late. In Palestine she joined a group of young people who determined to go back to Europe and rescue Jews now fatally trapped. Senesch parachuted back into Hungary and was immediately caught, tortured, and killed. Her bravery is not in question. We needed fighters but did we need this useless sacrifice at a time when each Jewish life was endangered and each one saved a miracle? What sense was there in that sacrifice? It reeks of hopelessness and foolishness. Is it all right that her mission failed because she was a girl? Did the facts of World War II later lead us to make some unconscious equation of Jew and female, the weaker sex, the second sex and the second people? Perhaps. It seems that Hannah Senesch has become celebrated because of the intense Jewish need to create a heroic mythology around the disaster. The story of Hannah Senesch is meant to work as a kind of opposing antidote vision to the lines of Jews waiting for trains that would take them to their death. By selecting a girl for this role, the community manages to avoid the painful fact that the Jewish male was unable to defend his family and it emphasizes the weakness of the Jews at that time by identifying the Jews with a young girl. Hannah Senesch, subject to torture by the Nazis, has in the end only her moral virtue, her morality so superior to the evil Nazi. In this respect she becomes symbolic of the entire Jewish nation throughout the Holocaust. Unlike Saint Joan of Arc she did not have a single victory and unlike David who managed to defeat Goliath, this warrior lost everything. She is not as well known as Anne Frank and will probably soon be swallowed up as history provides us with other heroes and heroines. On the other hand her brief popularity occurred because her story does symbolize the moral tragedy of the time and underlines the only Jewish consolation which is moral integrity. Maybe Israel will produce for Jews a new Saint Joan.

Then there is Jewish Etty Hillesum, whose diaries are now widely read. She was a Dutch woman at the university, child of an assimilated family, involved in an affair with an older psychotherapist. She did not escape when offered the chance and ultimately embraced the suffering at Westerbork with a love of God and a desire to purify her soul. The writing is essentially that of a Christian martyr and the suffering, while it ended in the crematorium, along the way takes on a literary quality that is either lyric or artificial depending on one's taste. Once again the woman, the suffering woman, speaks for Jews and seems to offer some kind of redemption through her acceptance of God. This is a story that appears to uplift the soul. She was accepting of what God willed. She welcomed the pain He brought. This fits the Christian vision of sacrifice and it again makes the Jewish story into a religious parable, one that supports and does not threaten the religious view and one that places the power in the hands of God and so relieves humanity from the responsibility of its piles of children's eyeglasses, its mattresses full of human hair, its bodies starved, shaved, and gassed. The American publication of *The Diaries of Etty Hillesum,* not unsurprisingly, carries a quote from D. M. Thomas.

John Hersey, in *The Wall,* and Primo Levi, in *If Not Now, When?* have written about the resistance in Warsaw and the Jewish partisan groups that fought and survived in the woods of Poland and Russia. Historians Emanuel Ringelblum and others have chronicled many brave acts of resistance. Nevertheless their courageous lives do not in our memory balance the weight of the tragedy. This is a historical experience that does not have colossal heroes, because the defeat was so monumental.

The most moving and direct Holocaust book of all remains Elie Wiesel's *Night,* which tells facts, simply, clearly, and without room for question. Like a prayer it makes its own sound and the sound of all the others to whom the prayer belongs. The power of the book lies in its purity. Its clarity. Its truth, its control over grief. Its lack of sentimentality. The importance of witnessing is stressed over and over again in the writings of survivors who try to catch every detail, who promised themselves they would tell the world, they would not let the dead go into oblivion, or the crime go unmentioned. The desire to tell it all comes to artists like Primo Levi who brings to the subject reason and precision and science and irony and grace and who makes us familiar with murder. The control of Levi's writing, the control of his mind, the rationality that the Enlightenment had celebrated and encouraged, becomes in his pages a mockery, a hot fire that burns just underneath the grid of his tight prose and threatens not the writer but the world with explosion.

Ordinary people with ordinary gifts also witnessed. They remember the moment they received their tattoo, the shaving of the hair, the long hours of standing in the heat and the cold and the train rides without water that ended in the rush to the crematoria. Hundreds of such books are now in print. The pen is mightier than the sword only when one has no sword. The Jews at least had a pen: too late to save a single soul but in time to bear witness, to take comfort from the revenge of telling, of speaking aloud, of backward prophecy which is better than no prophecy at all.

The survivors fulfilled their promises by writing. The generation of survivors can at least know they will have left behind them the story. It is as if Isaac could have told us how he felt on the way to Mount Moriah, as if Jesus told us how it was on the cross and what he wanted us to remember of his experience. The survivors' stories eventually became commonplace. Now there is a surfeit and publishers are mostly unwilling to take more. Private presses are still printing survivors' books and in manuscript form many are passed back and forth among families. Some survivors have written down tales for their children and grandchildren, some have photocopied these papers and sent them to friends and acquaintances. The pure telling of it is almost over, as the survivors reach the end of their lives. The telling of the story provides a modicum of revenge as when a child whispers to her bullying older brother, "I'll tell on you." But in this case the witnessing very often has not served to relieve the survivor of his burden. The list of Holocaust writers who take their own lives grows longer each year: Adorno, Nelly Sachs, Tadeusz Borowski, Paul Celan, Jean Amery, and now Primo Levi.

Holocaust material seems not to be controlled or transformed by writing. André Schwartz-Bart ends his novel *The Last of the Just* in a kind of affirmation of martyrdom, but we close the pages filled with images of brutality and despair. Readers are not left in an affirming condition. Art did dare to be more than silent. It did make knowable that which had been unknowable. It used language, in new ways, to express the violation of language and life that had occurred, but in the end, art, unlike the crucifixions and pietàs of Renaissance painting, could not lift the soul. It could only describe the existing conditions. Holocaust writing, whether of first quality or not, remains informational, testimonial, prophecy. Those of the Holocaust books that are true literature, Wiesel, Levi, Appelfeld, have found their art in their negation. They tell us what Anne Frank could not: the truth. These books are masterful. The language is right, the form is right, and yet the books are never just literature, they are always history, they are always accusations, indictments of the human condition. Do Christians read those books? Some do, of course, but the majority do not.

They do read Anne Frank and are reassured, at bottom, after everything, people are basically good.

The writers, the real writers, survivors and others, did more than witness, they attempted to be judge and jury, to reason with the unreasonable, to balance the tale so that it could be absorbed into human experience, so that it could serve as a warning, as a prototype, as a prayer, as a metaphor for destruction, as a simile for the death of civilization, as stories that might themselves civilize, as the myths of the Greeks were intended to do, as the stories of the Torah were intended to do, as the tale of the Crucifixion and the Resurrection was intended to do. The fact that these Holocaust stories in all likelihood will no more stay the savage hand than did their predecessors cannot be helped.

Some movies have been made that are extraordinary artistic contributions to our knowledge and understanding of the Holocaust. The films like the books are almost always understated, muted, told indirectly, filled with the unsaid and the unseen. We have *Night and Fog, The Pawnbroker,* and *The Shop on Main Street,* as well as the documentary films *Shoah* and *The Sorrow and the Pity,* but much of the Holocaust writing by screen and television writers often falls to the level of cartoon, and while this is offensive to some it is not so much a desecration as a search for the drama, an easy quick use of the metaphor that Appelfeld speaks of. The Holocaust as entertainment should not be shocking in a world in which the Passion plays have drawn large audiences, in which entertainment has always been one of the functions of the religious structure, and morality, however oversimplified, has always been depicted through characters wearing masks, divided into good and evil. Holocaust entertainment at least manages to convey to the general public some of the basic historical facts and for that alone we should be grateful.

We have learned that silence will not come until after the final disaster when there are no more human voices left to tell the story. We have learned that forty or maybe fifty years after an event there can still be fresh art coming from new sources that have not yet spoken. We know that art is never a thing unto itself but always a moral act, because it extends our capacity to feel for others, it gives us the means to understand landscapes we have never seen, because it always functions against the totalitarian state. When Holocaust artists speak it is already too late. However, the good work, the best of it, may be just in time to illuminate the abuses that lie ahead.

The differences between Jewish and Christian views on the Holocaust will continue to appear in books, in films, in historical accounts. The Jewish versions will continue to contain a direct or indirect accusation and the Christian creations will continue to place the emphasis on universal suffering and cosmic perspectives.

Today the Jew is this mixture of rage without satisfaction, a figure whose existence, whose persistence, reminds of the world's evil, worse than a hunchback who simply reminded of God's accidents and so was supposed to give luck, worse than a beggar who reminds of poverty, the Jew, no matter how successful, how talented, how secure in his place, reminds the Christian of innocence lost, of moral collapse, of social illness that may have been terminal. The Jew then symbolizes all the massacres, all the unnecessary deaths in this most bloody century, and at the same time the Jew worries the Christian: what of vengeance now? The Jew makes the Christian angry: so angry some are willing to bury the facts under lies. The Jewish victimization, with its preservation of moral integrity, disturbs some Christians so much that they welcome the recent turn of Israel-Arab events that has placed Jews in apparently compromising positions. When Jews are no longer the meek and the vulnerable, they become immediately the target of old angers. This is a thicket in which people of goodwill can easily lose their bearings. This is the thing that has not yet healed: that is within us still.

God After the Holocaust

Here is a story about an old Hasid. He is sitting in his study praying when he feels a pain in his chest and sees his whole life passing before him. In the background there is desert stretching out to the horizon's edge and at every milestone of his life, his birth, his brith, his bar mitzvah, his wedding, he sees two sets of footprints in the sand, which he understands as his and God's. But at the tragic points of his life, sickness, the death of his parents, the drowning of his only son, the death of his wife, only one set of prints is visible. Shading his eyes, to look for any sign of God's presence at these tragedies, he sees nothing, only one set of prints. Calling out to the Almighty he says, "Master of the Universe, where were you when I needed you most?" The voice of the Lord rolls out of the desert: "Don't you remember? I was lifting you up and cradling you so you could bear those moments."

A whimsical alibi, a story now rank with the innocence of other times, but a story that reminds us that the question of God's relation to pain on this earth is an old one and has not been newly discovered with the enormity of the Holocaust. But how it is answered, how it is tolerated, has changed for Jews with recent history. How God is understood or how Job is understood, whether or not the answers of the past will hold for the future, or whether new answers can be created is important, for while the Jews are a nation, a history, a culture, a tradition, a people, a memory, their religion, the one they held onto through inquisition after inquisition, the one that they passed on to their children knowing that it marked them for danger and limitation, is the glue, the sinew, the connecting tissue binding Jew to Jew, Jew to history. Without large numbers of the people, not all but a substantial core, believing and practicing the religion, the Jewish people could not and will not survive as a coherent entity. And the religion, despite the noble lyrics of such innovators as Mordecai Kaplan, may well dry up without God, a living God, who has much to answer for, whose past communications muffled in burning bushes and whirlwinds do not seem to answer today's questions for many in the community. Elias Canetti, writing in his notebook, says, "One cannot say 'God,' anymore. He is marked forever. He has war's mark of Cain on his brow . . ." But like most statements about God, this one is true for the writer but not for everyone. Many others can say God; many do. Despite the concern with the meaning of the Covenant with God after the Holocaust, Jewish life has, quite without reference to the ultimate aims of the cosmos or the indifference of the Creator, gone on.

When former Israeli prime minister Menachem Begin was asked by television reporter Gabe Pressman if he still believed in God, he said, "Sure I believe in God, God didn't let the Nazis win. He saved the Jewish people." This is selective vision at best. Or perhaps these are the words of a leader who knows that his people must have reassurances that all is well and God is bringing an end to human suffering. Is it possible that Noah made up the story of the dove with the olive branch to reassure his nervous family? Politicians who see rainbows whenever elections near are capable of an optimism that may escape the rest of us. But this is an optimism that most of us dearly want and deeply cherish. Richard Rubenstein, professor of religion at Florida State University, has said, "The hunger for superordinate meaning especially when confronting redemptive or catastrophic events would appear to be unquenchable. Indeed one sociologist of religion has argued with considerable cogency that religion is the audacious attempt to conceive of the entire universe as being humanly significant." We need religion, we will stand on our heads to make excuses for a Diety that appears to have betrayed us, we will try to avoid the issue of where He has been during our times of trial, even inventing charming stories of disappearing footsteps, and why not? We need religion for personal purposes, yes, but also for group survival.

The major branches of Judaism have each in its own way devised strategies to ensure the survival of the people. Dow Marmor, in his book *Beyond Survival,* points out that the Orthodox with their preoccupation with the past, with the exactness of tradition and ritual, are attempting to ensure that Jewish life continues, while the Reform are also trying to make it possible for Jews to remain Jews but live in the modern world. They are hoping through compromise to cut the rate of attrition: the loss to modernity. The Zionists are working to ensure the physical survival of the Jews in a political manner that will assure bodily safety. Marmor points out that without faith Jewish existence is dubious anyway. Without faith Orthodoxy becomes no more than compulsive rites and dries at its heart; without faith Reform surrenders to middle-class materialism, and loses its reason for being, and its children drift off anyway; Zionism can so easily, without a spiritual hand to steady the impulse, become an uncritical reliance on the might of the state, and a state without a Jewish spirit does not contribute to Jewish survival.

In the book of Jewish legends, the Taanith, this has been written: When the First Temple was about to be destroyed, bands upon bands of young priests with the keys to the Temple in their hands assembled and mounted to the roof of the Temple and called out, "Master of the Universe, as we did not have the merit to be faithful treasurers, these keys are handed back into your safekeeping." Then they threw the keys up toward heaven and there emerged the shape of a hand that received the keys from them. Whereupon the young men, crying and praying, leaped into the sky and sank into the tongues of fire below.

In the past when there have been Jewish defeats, Jewish catastrophes, the majority believed that the Jews themselves were, as their Prophets had told them, at fault. Their sins had brought punishment and the Lord looked away as the enemy approached, or He used the swords of cranky emperors to chastise his errant children. The fault was not God's but man's. This formulation was basic to the Jewish Covenant, and provided a strategy for Jews to continue as Jews even when things went badly.

But after the Holocaust the mingling of personal sin and historical destiny is no longer so easily accepted. The innocent died in numbers too great, the crimes of the people could not have earned such punishment: reason says so, compassion says so. Rabbi Irving Greenberg has said, "Let us offer no fundamental criterion after the Holocaust. No statement theological or otherwise should be made that would not be credible in the presence of burning children." Richard Rubenstein wrote in *Tikkun* magazine, "A generation ago this writer sadly concluded that the Jewish community's traditional mode of constructing a meaningful cosmos would only retain its credibility if the Holocaust were interpreted as God's chastisement of a sinful Israel. This entails seeing Hitler as a latter day Nebuchadnezzar and the death camps as God's method of punishment." This would violate Rabbi Greenberg's injunction and most of us cannot conceive of a way to bind sin, punishment, and Holocaust together. This strategy of blaming the people will no longer support Jewish survival.

Psychoanalyst Martin Bergmann said at a roundtable discussion of psychoanalysis and the Holocaust, "It's part of the Passover ritual to remember that in every generation there are persecutors out to exterminate us, but God saves us from them. The question is how long can you keep on saying that? How many Jews must die in order to still consider that God is saving us? Jews did not, like other nations, turn upon their God and accept the Gods of their victors. Rather they interpreted their defeats by saying to themselves, 'It is because of our sins that we are being punished.' Can we trust this process of internalization to go on and on? Is it still possible for a Jew to say, 'It wasn't God who was responsible, but us with our sins, and our sins were so great that we deserve six million dead?' "

At the same time that the relationship between God and His Chosen People might reasonably have fallen on hard times, the 1980s have seen an increasing number of young people returning to the Jewish religion, it has seen a revitalization of synagogues all across America. The Orthodox movement which might have been expected to wither away, since it depends heavily on the relationship between disobedience of God and personal and communal destiny, has instead increased its strength sevenfold. When the daughter of the Muncascer rabbi was married recently in New York,

20,000 guests came to the wedding at the Jacob K. Javits Center, and this is a Hasidic group that was nearly wiped off the face of the globe by the advancing Einsatzgruppen. If some of us have trouble trusting the God who chose the Chosen People, others have found ingenious ways around the problem, have not seen the problem at all, have needed God with such a thirst that they were willing to swallow anything, to leap in acts of desperate faith across the crematoria.

Dr. Martin Bergmann said, "As psychologists we can only say that there is a very powerful process of internalization that maintains the idealization of God at all costs, the way the young child maintains the idealization of the parent." What this means is that the child whose mother burns her face and arms with a cigarette needs her mother so badly that she cannot allow herself to despise or reject her parent and so the anger she feels, the explanation she looks for, settles on herself, and she assumes she must be a bad girl, an unworthy girl, a girl who should be punished. This way she remains a child who still has a good mother, which is her first necessity. Are the Jews in this sense like abused children?

The Holocaust, by making Jews feel threatened, vulnerable, in need of protection, has also thrust them back toward their God, in hopes that the next time He will save His people. The Holocaust increases a religious need because of the implicit need to justify the deaths that occurred, to justify the meaning of being Jewish. If there is no God, no Judaism, then how much more pointless the suffering, how much more unbearable becomes the Jewish portion of history. If there is a God and a purpose, then all can be borne by the nation as the Messiah, tarry though he will, moves toward us.

The Jews have another method of dealing with the trauma of the Holocaust and that is of submerging it, mingling it with the other disasters of their history, as David G. Roskies pointed out in his book *Against the Apocalypse*. This blending of history into myth has been the time-honored Jewish technique for swallowing their difficult history and understanding the painful present. The disaster of the two temples becomes one liturgical disaster and lamentations cover both events. Jews, as Yosef Yerushalmi has pointed out in his book *Zakhor,* are not so much historical, a people interested in keeping the exact record of their progress through the world, as they are liturgical, seasonal, involved with religious memory, with myth and its revelations, the group destiny rather than the particular, the group experience as it conforms to the master plan of exile and redemption: not as random lines straggling forward in time.

And indeed the Jews have had plenty of precedence for disaster. They can add the Holocaust, simply another along the way, to the long line of history that they see as an extended wait for the Messiah. We have slavery in Egypt, redemption . . . destruction of the First Temple . . . redemption . . . destruction of the Second Temple . . . partial redemption in the work of the rabbis who preserve Judaism in exile; we have the Spanish Inquisition, the Portuguese expulsion, the expulsion from England, the Crusades, the Khmelnitsky pogroms of the seventeenth century, the Ukrainian pogroms of 1901–1903, the pogroms of 1918, 1919, and into this list we add the Holocaust and the redemption, the return to the land of Israel. This is history but it reads like the stars turning around the globe, repetition, seasonal disaster, death and rebirth over and over again. The Jews have used their past to mourn their present and this form of lamentation has become so familiar that it has allowed the Jewish people to absorb blow after blow in the belief that history has a message for Jews, or Jews are carrying the message of history, Jewish history is the hieroglyphics of man, and that suffering has meaning on the route to redemption. Here is Shelomoh bar Shimshon writing about the murder of the Jewish community in Mainz during the Crusades as reported by Yerushalmi in *Zakhor:* "Who has heard or seen such a thing? Ask and see. Has there ever been an Akedah [the binding of Isaac on Mount Moriah], like this in all the generations since Adam? Did eleven hundred Akedot take place on a single day with all of them comparable to the binding of Isaac, son of Abraham? Yet for the one bound on Mount Moriah the world shook as it is stated, 'Behold the angels cried out and the skies darkened,' What did they do now, why did the skies not darken and the stars not dim . . . when . . . on one day . . . there were killed eleven hundred pure souls, including babies and infants . . . ? Wilt thou remain silent for these O Lord?" Despite the cry, the silence of the Lord was accepted, partially because there was a religious mythological framework already existing that could absorb the latest pain. The prayers for the dead of the pogroms of 1648 were used to include the dead of 1771 and on. The destruction of the First Temple was compared by the Psalmists to the fall of Sodom and Gomorrah, the Holocaust is called in Yiddish, Dir Dreiter Khurban, the Third Destruction, and our poet Yehuda Amichai evokes Sodom and Gomorrah when speaking of our fascination with the Holocaust as if we were Lot's wife. The disasters became not single events but consolidate themselves into a wheel of history that was expected to crush the Jew beneath so that he could be picked up next go-round: the lamentations are repeated again and again at the same time of year each year. In this way the Jewish mind has absorbed the shocks of 1,100 dead, of 11,000 dead, and is liturgically prepared to accept the new spoke in the wheel, the 6 million dead.

Our liturgy on Yom Kippur has included a prayer to the martyrs, and to those prayers at the Musaf service the Conservative Prayer Book has added prayers for the victims of the Holocaust. They include Rabbi Ismael, Rabbi Akiva, Rabbi Judah ben Hava, Rabbi Hanina ben Traydon, who were executed by the Roman courts. "These I recall and pour my heart out, How the arrogant have devoured us." The prayer book goes on to remember the Jewish girls of Warsaw who were violated by the Nazis and a child who wrote a poem in Terezin and includes a piece by Soma Morgenstern, a survivor, that offers prayers to God while reproaching Him with His silence: "If the prophets stood up in the night of mankind like lovers who seek the heart of the beloved night of mankind would you have the heart to offer?" This is written in the same language and tone as the rest of the prayer book. The line between Akiva and the Warsaw Ghetto remains unbroken. The Holocaust is then one more disaster in a list that may not have ended, but becomes inextricably bound with Jewish purpose, sin, and redemption. What else is Yom Kippur about? For some people this is a theological solution, for others it is a theological absurdity.

There has also been, as David Roskies tells us, a countercurrent throughout Jewish history, a form of using mockery of God, of taunting Him for His failure to save the Jews, by inverting or playing with the lines of the liturgy. This too has been going on a long time. Roskies quotes from the Jewish text, B. Gittin B6 56B: "Who is like You among the mute since He sees the suffering of His children and remains silent." This bitter remark he finds in Aba

Hanan, a Tanna of the second century: "Who is like You mighty in self Restraint?" He finds this in the texts after the Crusades: "There is none like you among the dumb, keeping silence and being still in the face of those who aggrieve us."

This form of complaint to God, because it still uses the language of the Bible, maintains the connection of God with the people even while releasing the anger that must have been there all along, that did not develop suddenly with the Nazi boot, but grew throughout the springtime ritual murders, the pogroms of the eastern slopes, the burnings at Blois, the massacre at Mainz, the long history of martyrdom and oppression in exile. The anger and bitter disappointment in God we hear in these words were certainly felt by generations of young Jewish intellectuals who were called to Socialism, to Communism, to a life of art and literature and science and left behind the people to mourn former catastrophes while waiting for new ones. However, the enormity of the Holocaust is such that it seems almost beyond human complaint and use of biblical language and imagery is now such that it chokes in the throat. Here is Dan Pagis's poem: "Here in this carload I am Eve with Abel my son; if you see my other son, Cain, son of man, tell him that . . ."

While it is clear that the State of Israel was established as a form of world atonement after the Holocaust, no one has suggested that one was worth the other, and while a return to the Promised Land would seem to be a redemption, if a complicated one at that, very few feel as confident as Begin that God saved the Jews and brought them once again to the Promised Land of Israel. For many the problem between God and His Chosen People persists.

In order for this conflict to be resolved, a new understanding must be reached on the meaning of Jewish suffering. The deaths of the six million must be organized into a meaningful cosmos, they must have a purpose other than random cruelty, and it will not work simply to pick up the old answer, Jews were being punished for their sins: that for the vast majority of Jews simply won't hold anymore.

"What is the purpose of Jewish suffering?" In "The Assistant," Bernard Malamud's character Frank Alpine asks the owner of a small grocery store, Morris Buber. The poor grocer answers the Italian, "We suffer for you." This Christian idea (expressed by a Jewish writer who could think of no other answer for the question), that one can take on the pain of another, can suffer punishment to spare the other punishment, to teach the other something, to become the crucified as a method of conveying God's message to man, is another attempt to give meaning to the fate of the six million, to the pain of the Jews in this world. This is not an entirely new strategy to preserve both Jewish worth and God's role in human affairs. David Biale points out that Judah ha-Levi, the great Spanish Jewish poet and philosopher, suggested in appropriation of the Christian motif that the suffering and humiliation of the Jews are a sign of God's continual election; powerlessness becomes a virtue, the meek shall inherit the earth, the crucified one is the beloved son of God, the heir, the voice on earth of the holy. The remark of Cardinal O'Connor that infuriated the Jewish leadership springs like a monstrous child out of this tradition. The cardinal, trying to make sense of the murders at Auschwitz, said that the Jewish suffering was a gift to the world. This idea of the pain of one being an offering for the other's soul is a Christian thought and one that brings a bitter taste to the Jewish mouth after all that has happened. It is another one of those things that cannot be said in front of burning children, and even if it gives meaning to the catastrophe, the meaning is so vicious that most could not accept a God who designed such a display of chosenness, such an election, such a parade of pain for the gain in virtue of the other nations.

The allied mythological system that attempts to save the Holocaust from absurdity is the connection of sacrifice to the burnt offerings of the camps. Here we start with the Akedah and go on to the sacrifice of the son of God, Jesus Christ, and from there to the sacrifice of the greater part of Jewry in a line of increasing violence. This emphasis links the murder of children to the will of God whose intention was to bring the human race closer to redemption. We can fit into this mythological line the eating of his children by Cronos and the destruction of Cronos by his son and follow on to the casting out of Oedipus and the murder that results. While this doesn't explain the Holocaust, it does reveal our human need to murder our children, or to have God do it symbolically for us, to have God save us from murdering our children by offering His own. This constellation of ideas that formed the base of great religions cannot contain the realities, the details of hair and teeth and bodies in ditches, and children's necks broken and furnaces going twenty-four hours a day. The binding of Isaac had a happy ending. The Crucifixion had a joyous resolution if only in eternity, but the story of the Holocaust offers no hereafter and so it cannot carry the weight of our need for redemption, for meaning, for purpose on this weary globe.

The theologian-writer Arthur A. Cohen spent years working on this philosophical problem. He said after Auschwitz, "I dearly hope I can reconstruct if not the old terrain (hardly likely) then some new ground upon which we stand and still bow our heads before the great God." He wanted to succeed with all the fervor of his innately religious soul. We are most of us still there, with Arthur Cohen in the dilemma he never solved, afraid to be without God because of the emptiness and chaos that brings, afraid because the Jews will not survive without God, although they have had a hard enough time surviving with Him. We are in need of God because we have a need for meaning; even when we shout out that we don't, even when we chant our bravado, our anger with God, we are still in need and this need has driven part of the Jewish community back into the synagogues to pray as Jews have always prayed just as if the covenant still stood as it had with Abraham and Isaac, just as it was when Moses stood on the mountaintop peering wistfully into the Promised Land. The facts of the matter have led other Jews away from the synagogues, away from prayer into a corner where they abide uncomfortably with the face of history. Those Jews hold their anger up to examination, but they too are not content. How could they be?

Anger with God goes out into the air and never finds its mark. It tends like the boomerang to return to its sender, to return to the heart and cause difficulty, human to human, to release itself in our ordinary daily conflicts between Jew and Jew, Jew and Christian, black and white, nation against nation. The anger against God, against a God that cannot be there, or has broken His word, or has demanded too much, is very much a Jewish constant in this post-Holocaust world.

Rabbi Emil Fackenheim, professor of philosophy, after carefully examining the broken promises of God, the fact that Jewish sinfulness can no longer explain Jewish suffering, feels that Judaism as it existed in the Galut is over. But Jewishness, Judaism, he believes will survive its own demise. He comes to the conclusion that Jews must remain Jews, which means they must continue to believe in some way, simply to survive, to defy the enemy, to assert the power of the group over those who would have exterminated them all. This idea appeals to our self-regard, to our desire to remain on the globe. It reinforces our sense of communal worth and necessity, but it does not, after the first glow, quite support the weight of Jewish life and the pain of Jewish destruction. We cannot go on just to show someone we haven't been killed. We need more positive and more complicated reasons. To defy evil is fine, but that defiance sends only a bright flare into the night. It stokes only a small fire. It cannot send warmth down the aeons.

The odd thing about Jews, atheists, and agnostics, secularists, Freudians, humanists included, is that the anger with God survives the disbelief in the Diety. The power of the words of the Covenant are so strong, imprinted in Jewish childhood, learned through the great power of the High Holidays, through the literature that is the Bible, through the words of the Prophets, through the echoes in poetry and art of all civilization, that even when the Jew says, "No, I don't accept this Covenant, this God in the Whirlwind who tortured Job for pages and reconciled him in a few words," even then the anger lingers, as if the God whose majesty and omnipotence is no longer believed is still to blame, is still a player in the drama. Instead of praise, this God is now assumed to be imaginary, invented by man, and is nevertheless accused with as much bitterness as if there were no doubt about his actual reality. This is not logical but it is so.

God not only failed to save most Jews but He failed to exact vengeance. It says in the Book of Psalms. "He will execute Judgement upon the nations and fill the world with corpses. He will shatter the enemy's head over the wide earth." The economic miracle that is West Germany turns the Psalmist into a buffoon, a jester in the court of the Nazis. The handful of old men who have been brought to trial only emphasize the many who lived their lives in physical comfort, in communal honor, in towns in Argentina, Peru, Mexico, in Düsseldorf and Hamburg, and Great Neck and Winnetka. The skies did not darken at the time and they did not darken afterward. Jean Amery, the Belgian writer and survivor, reported that in Auschwitz a practicing Jew once told him, "Your civilization and your intelligence are worthless but I have that certainty that God will avenge us." That's a helpful certainty, and Amery states that it aided the speaker to survive as it supported his spirit during times that might otherwise pulverize the soul, leading to the body's capitulation. But rescue came too late for most and revenge, if it was God's responsibility, His role in the play, never came at all. Another reason for Jewish anger with God.

Martyrdom, the principle of Kiddush Hashem, to die for the sanctification of His name, was invoked by various rabbis before the pits, before the crematoria, as they spoke to their congregations, congregations about to be murdered. Martyrdom while not overvalued in the rabbinic tradition, nevertheless has been a thread, a minor theme in Jewish history. We remember the mother of the pious boys who preferred the death of her children to their conversion. We remember Rabbi Akiva who was burned with the Torah wrapped around him, Rabbi Ben Harkeness who was killed for teaching Torah, and we make heroes out of those who died for their faith. The Catholic Church does a more thorough job than we do with this. They make saints, paint pictures of torture, and have angels who carry off the dead to a better world. The Jewish stories seem to end at death, and while the martyrs are given due respect they are hardly venerated, prayed to, or even immortalized in stone. The closest Jews came to group martyrdom prior to the Nazi period was at Masada, and there as with the other martyrs there was some element of choice: arms had been taken up, rebellion was under way, a decision to defy authority was made. This was different than standing, wholesale communities, naked at the edge of a ditch where death was to come, not because of defiance of the state, but because of the fact of Jewishness; a Jewish parent or even grandparent alone was the death warrant. Rabbi Daniel of Kelme spoke on the meaning of Kiddush Hashem as the crowd of women and babies, old and young, stood before the trenches waiting for the shooting to begin. One can admire, one can understand his attempt to make sense out of the barbarity at hand, but the fact is that these were not sanctifications of the Name in the traditional sense, and if God had called for them, accepted them as such, what kind of God would He be? The concept of Kiddush Hashem may have comforted some on the way of dying, but for many in the modern world this is only a pathetic attempt to explain, to place in a familiar religious framework, events which destroy that framework, which cannot be forced to give meaning or dignity to human action.

The ancient martyrs, after all, always had choice: they could have converted, laid down their arms, stopped teaching Torah. The victims of the Nazi genocide could do nothing to avoid their fate. They were offered no choices. This cannot be martyrdom as the world, Jewish and non-Jewish, has understood it, incorporated it into religion and history and art. Of course the whole of Jewish history has the flavor of martyrdom about it. The people themselves, the mass of people, have been hounded, burned, exiled, pillaged, and ultimately nearly exterminated. This may be why Jews are less fond of martyrs than Catholics. For Catholics these are inspiring stories of noble spirits, for Jews these are tales that represent the fate of the people, the nation in this world not the next.

But the need for belief goes on. Jewish identity, Jewish survival, is at stake and so some preserve their belief, some have come to adopt a nonquestioning stance as a means toward an end: the end, the survival of the Jewish people which has become for them a vital matter of necessity, the only revenge left. Here is Aharon Appelfeld, a man who describes the ominous and bewitched world of the assimilated prewar Jew in a Europe that had stretched the art of civilization so thin that it was about to tear apart. He himself fled the concentration camps as a child of eight and survived by his wits among the peasants and the partisans. His family, the world he had known, vanished. In the *Baltimore Jewish Times* he says: "Today I can't imagine myself as a Jew without being religious. It's individualistic religion, one I made my way to . . . but I can't imagine any form of Jewish life without prayer and the synagogue. I came to that because after looking inside myself, I felt there is meaning to life, even after Auschwitz, and so there is the obligation to continue. If there is meaning, then there is God. Faith gives us a chance. It is up to us what to do with it." The hunger for meaning, especially after the destruction, is so great that some must have it. They grant it to themselves. They hold their questions in abeyance. They construct elaborate philosophical arguments that take the power away from God to interfere in the fate of men but leave Him with the capacity to love man, the capacity to hear without immediate response the prayers that are offered. Theologians are working on theories of an imperfect God who needs man to complete Him, to fulfill Him. This is a version of Cabalistic thought that allows man to participate in the divine unfolding. It removes the power of God from the heavens while preserving the mystery, the spiritual, the longing for God that is undoubtedly human. This is fine for those it convinces, for whom the majesty remains, but for others, a less than all powerful God is like Eeyore without his tail, an endearing but rather pitiful and grouchy creation. Some can go on worshiping a Diety that broods in the heavens tending His own imperfections, watching His own limitations. Some construct arguments that excuse God or engage Him in a dialogue. Others, abandoning logic for emotional truth, complain about His absence in books, in plays, in movies, and occasionally we complain directly to God himself about His silence, His ineffectiveness, His disappearances, His nonexistence. Is He really cradling us in His arms at the difficult moments of our lives or are we masters of self-levitation?

So Jews are left, those who still accept the Covenant of the Torah as it has always been, those who cannot accept it the way it was but have no other way to offer, with anger, anger that is open or hidden, anger that is directed at God, or turned toward man. Many Jews live with anger and disappointment, disappointment so deep that it becomes the primal sea out of which more anger rises.

In order for us to reduce this anger we must first face it in all its ugliness. We may not find theological peace and it may well take centuries before the lines of the religion readjust themselves to the reality of human history, but for now, at this time, we can only be patient with each other, understanding of those who have not forgiven God, not enough to return to synagogue, and patient and understanding of those who have managed to leap across the impossible questions and reap the comforts that a deep faith brings.

For Christians there was of course no betrayal of covenant, but some must wonder where was Jesus with his mercy and his healing hand. For Christians there is the troubling question of the corruption of those raised as Christians who lost their moral way. For Christians the Holocaust is not a theological crisis but a discomfort. If the Jewish God is in question, then the Christian God is also threatened: the tradition after all has deep interconnections. So we struggle and wonder and grow angry with each other for having easy answers or no answers or the wrong answers. This is a time when many of those who would love God suffer some pain.

Blacks and Jews

A LOST FRIENDSHIP

The Reverend Louis Farrakhan called Judaism a "gutter religion," branded Jews as "sharks," and warned them not to assume they could escape another Holocaust. He said, "You can say 'never again,' but when they put you in the ovens, never again don't mean a thing." Here he struck a raw nerve, and Jews have responded with anger and bitterness.

It is no secret that some blacks have been openly anti-Semitic and anti-Zionist. As Jews respond to the provocation by turning their back on their former friends they become the enemy of equal opportunity, the enemy of pluralism in this country, the enemy of the democratic process that is intended to create the best society possible for the majority of its people: as such we cut off our nose to spite ourselves, we fall once again for the illusion that if they like us at court we are safe, a position that has historically proved erroneous, a temporary balm at best. If Jews lose connection with the black person or the impoverished person, then Jews become newest broken link in the American Dream. Jewish self-interest depends on that American Dream, on its pluralism, on its openness. The more tolerant and gracious to strangers the society becomes, the safer the Jewish place within: that is clear enough.

It is a fact that Jews were in the forefront of the civil rights movement. There is the famous picture of Rabbi Abraham Joshua Heschel, long-bearded, heavy, dark coat, walking arm and arm with Martin Luther King as the line of protesters approached the outskirts of Selma. We remember Michael Schwerner and Andrew Goodman, Jewish sons of American liberals, their bodies discovered under the bridge in rural Mississippi with James Chaney, a black colleague; all murdered by white southerners whose only dreams were nightmares. There were thousands of unknown Jewish lawyers working in NAACP headquarters in places where the papaw season went on for months, places far from the Lower East Side where their parents and grandparents had read the *Forward* and talked of anarchists and Trotskyites over a glass of tea at the local dairy restaurant. Black activists, the Stokeley Carmichaels and the Andrew Youngs, once raised money by the barrelful in the living rooms of Great Neck and Scarsdale: in the living rooms of Jewish manufacturers, Jewish doctors and dentists, investment bankers, sons and grandsons of pushcart peddlers, of Yiddish-speaking immigrants who had never seen a "shvartzer" till the boat landed. Martin Luther King said that more than 90 percent of the checks over one thousand dollars he received came from Jews.

It is also true that all that has ended. Polls show that anti-Semitism, on the wane all across America, is increasing only among blacks. The polls show that among educated blacks anti-Semitism is rising higher each year. Black leadership, with the possible exception of the extraordinary David Dinkins and a few others, would not publicly reject Farrakhan. Populist politics required silence. Morality as usual, conscience as usual, was engaged in washing its hands. In addition presidential candidate Jesse Jackson removed some planks from the bridges between the two minorities when he threw his arms around Yasir Arafat, when he spoke of

"Hymietown," when he refused to disavow Farrakhan firmly.

During the 1988 presidential primary in New York City, Mayor Ed Koch, tilting his head at the cameras, adopting his, but I'm just a sweet kid whose seen hard times in the mean streets: bad boy with heart-of-gold expression, said, "Jews would have to be crazy to vote for Jesse Jackson." He expressed a sentiment widespread in the Jewish community and one that both reflected the racial tensions already existing and turned the heat up higher, metamorphosing presidential politics into a street fight of my guys against yours. As Jackson ran for president we saw the Jews uneasy, nervous, unwilling to accept an apology for Hymietown, unwilling to believe that Jackson is not a friend of Arafat's who would sell out Israel in his first moments of power, unwilling to believe that his Rainbow Coalition is sincere. The Farrakhan matter is so frightening to Jews that it becomes impossible for many to see Jackson, caught in his own political necessities, only a politician after all, not a saint. Jackson extends the hand of friendship to Jews but does not slap the Palestinian face in so doing. At the moment the Jews are too leery of betrayal, too determined to defend themselves, too afraid of compromise to trust him. The Holocaust created Jews unwilling to trust, unwilling to compromise their interests, to assume the best, to tolerate insult. The blacks will remember this opposition, and the anti-Semitism that might otherwise have passed with other fads and fashions will spread, rise to epidemic proportions as their leader is opposed by Jews. The *Amsterdam News* said on its editorial page, "For Black America Jesse Jackson has brought pride and a sense that there is something that we can do about our plight in America." If Jews are finally perceived as the enemy of the leader of the black people, it will take the Messiah himself on his first or second visit to bring the two peoples back together, and if Ed Koch really represents the Jewish view of the American political scene then the politics of self-interest will have supplanted the politics of idealism for Jews, and if Jesse Jackson is the Moses of the poor people of this nation and Jews are the Goliath that appears to prevent them from residing in the Promised Land then the real racists and bigots, safe in the stands, will surely consume all the milk and honey themselves, while watching the gladiators of the day do each other in.

The friendship that once was so firm suffered a heavy blow as Jewish organizations spoke out against a legal quota system, a plan the black community was counting on to alleviate the effects of discrimination and poverty. This anti-affirmative-action stand only confirmed in the black community images of Jewish greed and political power. Jewish money for black causes disappeared and scholarships were left dangling in the air. The two communities split over the matter of the Palestinians: terrorists or displaced persons? The breach is still there despite the attempts of the late black civil rights leader Bayard Rustin, leaders of the American Jewish Committee, the American Jewish Congress, other elder statesmen of both groups, to cover the divide with artificial turf. Rainbow coalitions can only appear after the rains have stopped, and at this time the weather conditions have not changed. It can be said that the Jews were concerned and identified with the interest of Negroes but changed their minds when the Negroes became blacks. It can be said that the blacks were friendly enough to Jews when they needed their money and their blood to arouse the conscience of a drowsing America, but that when it was more convenient to ally with the Third World, they proved fair-weather friends, only too willing to turn when the political moment seemed opportune: only too eager to have their own scapegoats to blame. What was the Holocaust if not a mass lynching, and none of us deny that it is more comfortable to be a member of the crowd that stands at the base of the tree than the one that swings in the breeze.

The Holocaust itself became a sore point between blacks and Jews, probably as a symptom of the serious divisions already existing between the two groups and not as an original cause of the enmity. The Holocaust offers us one thread that we can use to find our way through the unfortunate maze of black-Jewish conflict. Jews insist that the Holocaust is a unique event in modern history, unparalleled in its horror by any other, unequaled in its depravity and obscenity by any other. Blacks find this view egocentric, or tribal-centric. They feel it ignores or erases their own suffering and the atrocity done to them in the eighteenth and nineteenth centuries. Those centuries brought the wondrous spread of civilization and the benefits of the Enlightenment only if your skin was white. Blacks talk about the cargo ships that brought the slaves to the New World; what is the difference between the hold of a boat in which thousands perish on a voyage to slavery and the railroad car packed with those destined for death and enforced labor: what makes your tragedy of greater significance than ours? Toni Morrison dedicated her novel *Beloved* to "sixty million and more." The reference to the Jewish six million is clear.

The Jews have managed to make the Holocaust into one of the most talked-about, central issues of modern times. The blacks have written and spoken of the crime of slavery, of the death ships, of the effects on culture and family of slave institutions for years, and yet the Holocaust as symbolic embodiment of evil, with monuments and museums, by presidents' special councils, and memorial days, has come from behind to take center stage. Jewish organizations and Jewish writers and Jewish media people have overwhelmed the catastrophe of slavery with the more recent tales of the Holocaust. The argument: who has suffered more, who is more worthy of compensation, of special consideration in the world of real politics, of a central place in the sorrow of the human heart, is an argument to turn an angel stone-deaf. Whose tragedy was worse is hardly a prize anyone wants to vie for—and yet between blacks and Jews the competition for the disaster award rumbles on. It emits a toxic drip that erodes the once-unquestioned alliance between the liberal Jew who understood all too well the pain of the oppressed and the black who all too well understood what it was like to be different, to be a minority trapped inside a culture that doesn't want you.

The other root of black anti-Semitism echoes ironically within the old patterns of Eastern Europe, a design in which the Jews, themselves on the fringe of society, became the visible presence representing the absent landlords in the provinces, the moneylenders in the villages and the towns. Harlem in 1945, with its Jewish businesses that lined 125th Street, with its Jewish pawnbrokers, its Jewish landlords who came to the tenements and collected the rents, was all too similar to the villages and towns of the Old World in which the aristocracy managed to pit the Jews against the peasantry and step aside to watch as blood flowed. Jews have traditionally feared the uneducated poor, the workers and the peasants of Europe, because they, trading with and borrowing from the Jews, living cheek by jowl with the Jewish communities, pinched by the economic inequities that came from above, placed their resentment right at the Jewish door and often took out their frustrations with savage brutality on their unprotected neighbors. Here with the blacks, it is the same story, another economic dog with a Jewish bite. The Jewish Socialist who dared to defy his observant parents and run off into the anarchist night did so in order to help the peasant and the worker with whose pain he identified, whose situation he intended to change. He had a vision of a world of universal human kindness, one in which he and his family could belong. This vision, part self-serving, part altruistic, also prompted the children of the American Jewish dream to leave home and to sit in at lunch counters and spend time in front of county courthouses in Mississippi and Alabama in search of justice for all. These Jewish children found themselves within five years, like their cousins in czarist Russia, two generations before, and then again in the 1950s in Communist Russia, suspected, purged, singled out as members of a different religion, a group that could safely be despised. The list of grand humanistic, idealistic causes that have pulled in Jewish youth, only to spit them out again in revulsion, is long enough to make a history lesson or at least a two-column obituary for Brotherly Love.

This is not to deny that some Jewish landlords did indeed become slumlords or that some Jewish pawnbrokers exacted the last penny from the desperately poor, or that Jews became the holder of notes, the lender of the last resort in a place where the last resort usually came first. Jews, like other Americans, brought to capitalism some of the baser instincts, and the profit motive which is so extolled in the vice president of Chase Manhattan Bank can look a little shady in the push and shove of sofas bought on time and rents due on the first of the month. Some Jews did take the money and run to the suburbs, but other Americans were supplying black youth with drugs, were using them for cheap labor, for domestic work, for their consumer worth, and were living so high on the scale in places so distant and fine, like Tuxedo Park and Grosse Point, that blacks never even saw them.

The Jew is vulnerable to attack. His religion makes him a suspect in a dark passion play. He is near at hand. He can be hated without fear of repercussions. The Ukrainian peasants would have understood Farrakhan perfectly. His anti-Semitic diatribes are decorated with references to Jews and money. Jewish success in America, even when it had nothing to do with the black community, such as Jewish textile businesses, or professional status, aroused envy and anger. The assumption was made that in order to succeed, the Jew must have been extraordinarily crafty, greedy, and exploitive, more so than the far more successful older Gentile communities who were themselves preventing Jews from entering many areas of capitalist endeavor. This attitude toward the Jew and money is an old libel, one that confuses the middleman with the general, the flunky who delivers the order with the order itself. One that unites the entire beleaguered parish against the hated outsider. Nothing is as exhilarating, as unifying, as an enemy one can really hate. It inspires the troops, brings money to the cause, and distracts from failures of one's own. Hannah Arendt in *Origins of Totalitarianism* said, "As each class came into open conflict with the state they turned openly anti-semitic. So in Austria each nationality that came into conflict with the monarchy started its fight with an attack upon the Jews." The blacks of America gaining strength, beginning to create a political voice, they too have turned against the Jews. Hannah Arendt called the play from another country in another time. She saw it in the workers in Paris marching against Dreyfus. She saw it in the crowds on the streets of

Kiev that called for Bellis's head; a Jew accused of the ritual murder of a Christian child.

Anti-Semitism might not have transplanted so well to America's inner city had there not been other frictions between the two peoples. Among these lie the hard comparison between the success story of the Jewish immigrant and the hard-knock destiny of the black slave and his descendants. The Jewish immigrant came to this country with empty pockets, with a history of religious and racial persecution, backward by the standards of the community, believing in evil eyes and superstitious ritual, denied entry into European universities. Rare among the first enormous waves of Russian immigrants were those who were English-speaking, educated, ready to begin at the top. The vast majority were crowded into a ramshackle ghetto where appalling sanitation existed, where diseases flourished, and surviving meant working long hours at backbreaking labor. Like the blacks, they were an outsider group, a collection of poor souls who were not wanted or welcomed by any class of American society. They could never then have paid the toll on the highways that led to the corridors of American power and success.

The difference between the black community and the Jewish one, the slaves and the immigrants, is that attending the same public school systems, in Brooklyn and Queens, in Boston and Baltimore, going to the same movies in movie palaces in the Bronx and St. Louis: the Jews in one generation broke down the quota plan at Harvard, entered City College of New York in droves, and beyond the expectations of even the most optimistic of Founding Fathers, became a wealthy group that moved to the suburbs and complained of alienation and the rising cost of malpractice insurance. Over the years when many Jews were climbing as fast as possible, most blacks were standing still, their bright children were not tracked for college, their most enterprising and strong children, their most hardworking people, were denied promotion, opportunity for investment, for capital gain, denied access to the language and manners of American success. While some escaped the inner cities, many were left behind to stagnate in a culture that spoke another tongue, that had so different a style that it couldn't easily go downtown, that became further victimized by drug pushers, numbers runners, petty criminals who preyed on their own, the welfare system that never gave anyone enough for dignity and hope but nevertheless entered the bloodstream, a chronic disabling illness that is passed on from one generation to another, aided by a health care system that depersonalizes and makes tragic errors and allows an infant mortality rate among black newborns that if it appeared in Greenwich, Connecticut, would close the hospitals, strip the doctors of their licenses, and send the nurses to jail. Alcohol too has taken its toll. Too many fathers have become nonparents, leaving too many children to seek nourishment and protection in mean streets. In such an environment violence flows and numbers of young blacks are murdered each year in fights, with each other, with the police, with girlfriends. Crime and drugs, the handmaidens of poverty, have made the Horatio Alger rise from rags to riches a task fit only for Sisyphus whose tolerance for absurdity we all know.

American society has not found a way to help. It has turned its back and complained of the poor that are always with us, the unemployed that stay at an acceptable rate, corralled together in areas suitable for them, in overcrowded schools suitable for them, in housing that leaks and burns and crumbles. Neither Jews nor blacks were offered membership in established country clubs, but one group purchased its own fairways and built its own dance pavilions. Racism clearly blocked the black community. It has not yet found its own way out of the maze. The Jewish community has, and the difference is a source of anger for both groups.

This description is of course broad and it ignores the many Jews who have remained in poverty or near poverty and the many blacks who live in a substantial and lively middle-class environment, just not in large numbers, just not as organized, as economically visible as the Jewish one. The obvious explanation is racism. The explanation is that America was a land of opportunity except if your skin was of the wrong color. Black talent and achievement have gone unrecognized, unused, and the wasting of young minds and good gifts goes on and on. We know this is true and yet at the time the Jews moved forward, they too were excluded, disliked, looked down upon by all the powers that be. Some of the difference between the two groups is due to the different ability of each to use what little was offered, to take education in our public system and make of it opportunity for private enterprise and professional life. Of all the waves of immigrants who came to America with nothing at all, only the Jews quickly used the schools as ladders to climb the face of Miss Liberty. The blacks have dropped out of class in large numbers. They have been mistracked in schools and have underachieved consistently in comparison to other groups. They have not in large enough numbers left the language of the streets in the streets and learned the logic of the computer, the message of the microscope, the ticker tape of commerce. Racism in very subtle forms, some not yet clearly understood, has left us with a situation in which resentment must rise when peoples of equal inherent ability find such disparate fortunes in American life. The educated black particularly, the one who understands the value of education, turns on the Jew, not only a familiar target, one near at hand, but one who has caused pain by doing so well in bad times, starting with nothing and building so much, whose very success invites invidious comparison with those whose majority (never mind the complex external reasons) have not been able to turn their report cards into credit cards. It doesn't win friends for Jews to offer charity now to those who started at the bottom with them: what could be more enraging, more threatening to one's own dignity and self-worth?

There are rational nondemonic explanations for the different fates of Jews and blacks: the Jewish family came to this country poor but united, dedicated to the success of the children, prepared to sacrifice for the next generation. They were people of the Book, people who had always valued, perhaps overvalued, scholarship, study, anything that was called learning, all things that might cause you to end up wearing thick glasses, all things that might involve you in a technology of thought, in order to explain, expound, and accommodate the Law. The people of the Word were better prepared for modern life, for public school, for sitting long hours, turning the pages of heavy books in musty libraries, for the leap of faith, the play with ideas, that the mastery of science and business demands. The color of their skin permitted them to mimic, assimilate, pass into the American culture in larger numbers at faster rates. On the other side, slavery had destroyed family structures, it had pulverized individual and group pride, it had wounded a people of the field, broken their religion, and trampled their culture. Slavery ruptured an ancient and valued harmony of man and animal and nature and left its victims prey to all the diseases of urban disorder.

These explanations aside, one of the causes of tension between the two groups remains the differing fortune of the black and the Jew. I worked hard, says the Jew, I made it when the quotas were against me, and now you want to restore those quotas in your favor. That's not fair; and the Jew goes to his legislature, and he threatens to vote against his congressperson, and he writes a thousand articles in a thousand magazines. The black wants to move into a project in a better neighborhood where the Jews have fled from their own slums into a world of higher property values. The Jew takes to the streets and brings the TV cameras to focus on his placards. The black is forced to stay in his slum. Both groups have poured salt on each other's wounds.

And then there is the most serious matter of the Third World, the matter of the Palestinians: in American Jewish mythology the mantle of Hitler fell on the shoulders of Yasir Arafat. For the black a natural sympathy lies with the darker-skinned people of the Third World, with the displaced and distressed Palestinians who appear to be victims of the aggression of colonialist whites, never mind that these particular whites were themselves the victims of other even more virulent sorts, never mind that close to 60 percent of all Israelis are immigrants from Third World countries, with dark hair and olive skin. The lines are drawn sharply. The Jew is the friend of South Africa, the Evil Power with the guns and the bombs and the well-trained army, and the black has friendship for the one whom he identifies with, the one the others have chased out of the land and now use for cheap labor, for work that requires the bending of the back, or the sweeping of waste. Black pride and sense of place in the world are greatly enhanced by an identification with all Third World peoples. It is as reasonable for blacks to identify and care with political passion about the fate of peoples seen as victims of racist colonialism as it is for American Jews to fight furiously for the freedom of Soviet Jews. This matter of sympathy for the Palestinian, a confusion of racisms that belongs to South Africa, to colonialist Britain, France, and Germany, with fledgling Israel, a nation so new that never before have its people had an opportunity to bully anyone, at least not since ancient times, brings the matter of Jewish-black friendship right to the edge of the brink and perhaps over it.

Blacks felt that Jewish pressure caused Andrew Young to be fired from his position at the United Nations. Jewish political power, just like Jewish economic power, has always been overestimated. Jews were angry that Andrew Young had been so open in his leanings toward the Palestinians, but it is unlikely that Jewish clout alone could have removed him. Nevertheless, the incident increased tensions between the two groups and underlined the different alliances. Jewish power, mostly imagined Jewish power, became once again the match that started the fires of anti-Semitism.

Here we come back to the Holocaust. The Jews no longer allow the anti-Semitic comments of their neighbors to roll off their backs as they go about their business making their way over the obstacles we call our social system. Now when a Jew, any kind of Jew, assimilated, Orthodox, Socialist, Republican, what have you, hears the ranting of a demagogue, calling to his people to drive out the Jews, he responds with fury, with terror, with conviction that he has been truly threatened, that the words are more than an echo of an event, that they have the power to recall, to bring it on again, to repeat history. So Farrakhan, standing between his white-robed body guards and threatening the death of Jews, is not the ridiculous figure he might have been if we didn't all know, this is how it began once upon a time in the taverns of Bavaria. Jews now react to words like Hymietown, not the way they would in the thirties when one shrugged at the anti-Semitic comments of neighbors and coworkers and assumed they would suffer the effects of their own small-mindedness. In those days the Father Coughlins could be left to their own devices, they were familiar figures on a landscape that always had storms, little terrors that swelled and burst and turned the sky dark and went on. But now after the Holocaust no Jew hears words like Hymietown without summoning up the full panoply of disaster, the rails crisscrossing an indifferent Europe, the statesmen busy at their games, and the children selected and selected and selected.

Jews are so immediately aroused by the pictures in their heads that they forget the times they have used popular words to refer to blacks, the slurs that they have passed in jokes to one another, the casual remarks, the sense that blacks are other, strangers, even stranger than goyim, that Jewish humor reveals even if politeness would hide it. Jews are not innocent of antiblack feeling, of a racism that may run against the conscious grain but still has not disappeared. Jews who are indignant at the rise of anti-Semitism among blacks must know that some Jews have absorbed the racism that runs through American society and has made black progress even harder, slower, and more painful. If Jewish girls in the 1950s were changing their noses and straightening their hair, and they were, they were expressing the racism of the country. If Jewish people keep their neighborhoods white, or take their children out of public schools because of racial mix, then they are not innocent. In fact all groups harbor some ugly thoughts about the outsider. That is the nature of group: its joy and its terror.

The Holocaust also reminds blacks of what could happen to them, isolated, considered a different kind of human being, one not so human as all that. The black knowing the events of Europe in 1939–1945 does not doubt that man is capable of exterminating him. He does not believe that he can rely on the pillars and posts of civilization to hold up against any kind of flood. The black also knows that the Jews were the victims, and this makes him more likely to choose the Jew as his own object of hatred. They are already targets. They are the outsider's outsider, the pariah's pariah, even if recent life in America has disguised their vulnerability. Ah, what a sorry business this: two proud peoples, steeped in the history of struggle, turn not on the causes, abstract and concrete, that have plagued them. They turn instead on each other.

Recently a horror film opened called *The Believers.* In it an African cult is described: The Rule of the Yoruba Gods. The portrait of this religion in this movie is one of a group that kidnaps white children and sacrifices them to their God. The movie pictures a sinister black priest and presents all kinds of terrifying rituals as innocent white children are pursued through modern streets. This is just a movie, but it repeats the libel against Jews in the Ukraine, in Germany, in Poland. Jews were accused at Eastertime, at Passover, of using the blood of Christian children in a religious rite. The accusation was nonsense but it was widely believed. The Bellis trial in Russia was the result of such convictions. Jews have been killed because the populace accepted this fairy tale. Now the fact that it reappears in a horror film in the 1980s directed against blacks tells us that the basic primitive forms of prejudice, of superstition, of fear of the stranger, do not change. They bear all-too-familiar designs. Black and Jew know the result can be both slavery and holocaust. What a tragedy it would be if the Ani ma'amin (I believe in the coming of the Messiah even though he may tarry), the song of Jews through the ages, and the strains of "We shall overcome one day," remain in disharmony, mocking the purity of each.

In the American presidential election of 1984 the Jewish fears about Jesse Jackson appeared to threaten the traditional Jewish Democratic vote. In the end the Jews voted 60 percent Democratic and the pervasive dislike of Jesse Jackson probably did not sway many. Nevertheless the fact is that the division between black and Jew had threatened the old alliances and created a turmoil within the Jewish community. The Jewish Right has made an issue of Jackson and insisted that the real interests of the Jewish community, the interests of Israel, will best be served by the more conservative, militantly anti-Communist Republicans. Some Jews followed this line of thought easily. Since the exile in Babylon, Jews have been protected by the regent while their leaders were valued servants of the court. Ronald Reagan was running a court of sorts. Frightened of the turns that history might yet take, Jews of the Right felt that Jewish survival and prosperity depended on our being Esther in Ahasuerus's harem, of our abandoning dangerous subversive antistate positions that served the interests of other minorities within the general populace and consider only our own always precarious future, dance before the king for the survival of our people. Forget the others, they said, they don't like us, they don't owe us, and we don't owe them. The neoconservative Jewish Right called for an end to the old alliance of black and Jew. If we have incomes over 10,000 dollars a year, they asked, what are we doing with the minorities of this country?

This idea rumbled through the whole Jewish community: a Jewish doctor said at a dinner party to the assembled guests, "I don't care if little black chidren get free lunches or not, all I care about is what happens to the Jews." The statement rippled across the table, shocking for those of us who had always taken for granted that all Jews cared about the marginal, the weak, the ones who could not help themselves. The conversation turned to the president's policy in South America. "What about the anti-Semitism of the Sandinistas?" said the doctor. "What about the human rights abuses in Chile?" someone asked. "Chile," said the doctor, as if someone had named the capital of an Oriental kingdom that had sunk into the sea prior to the journeys of Marco Polo. "Chile? I am not political, like that, I care only what happens to the Jews." The guests gasped. The sound of splintering taboo filled the air. The rabbis in the Great Yavneh in the Sky, if they are there, put their hands over their ears.

The other Jewish guests at the dinner party did not agree, but the thought, the thought, had been said aloud and now it joined us at the table, genie out of the bottle, and while most of us did not approve, we had to allow it belonged among us. Why? The Haves are never happy to give anything to the Have-Nots. That is simple human nature. But this brand of Jewish self-interest is directly tied to the Holocaust. Because of the Holocaust the neoconservatives believed that we should be conservatives, neo or otherwise. Because, whether it is right or wrong, whether it is moral or immoral, it is far from foolish or simply mean to believe after the Holocaust that Jews who worry about the calories of little black children will end up with starving children of their own.

There is something else that runs through this problem, affecting our positions often without our complete conscious knowledge. Pride, Jewish pride, has been violated by the anti-Semitism of the world, which mocked and haunted Jewish life for centuries. Pride, Jewish pride, has been torn apart by the Holocaust. First we became so despised we were thrown out of the cultures of our homelands, then we were rounded up like animals and slaughtered like animals and humiliated because our God did not rescue us, our men could not protect their own, our virtues went up in smoke with our sins. We were the ones at the bottom, so far at the bottom we could be eliminated. In opposition to the trial of a suspected Nazi, David Kravine wrote in the *Jerusalem Post,* February 1986, "By trying Demjanjuk we expose our wounds to the stranger gaze. We thrust in their faces pictures of our collective humiliation." A generation and three-quarters later he still feels shame over the Jewish disaster. Now in America, even after Israel has flexed its muscle, after we have recouped, gained a prominent place in the universities, the businesses, the orchestras, and the art galleries of America, we still remember the bitter taste of former positions, the hurt both social and economic of centuries of anti-Semitism, the catastrophe that was the Holocaust. This is why it becomes psychologically attractive for some Jews to disassociate from the group in America that is branded by their skin as we were once branded by yellow stars and blue numbers.

This is why we may, good intentions aside, take rueful satisfaction that this trouble, this poverty, this racist disaster, is not ours, not our problem for which someone must seek a solution, even a final solution. Jews have a natural fear of losing what they have gained. In addition the unconscious is entitled to be ruthless and self-serving. Jews are not saints and will have the same joy at another's discomfort as affects all human animals from time to time. If some Jews want to feel identified with the secure and the wealthy in this country, with the Reagans riding their horses over the ample acreage of their country retreat, this we can understand. If Jews allow themselves to feel superior, to express disdain for others, they are healing old wounds, they are regaining lost pride: not the moral way to regain pride, but human enough, understandable enough.

In fact it is to the amazing credit of the large proportion of Jewish voters that they did not vote only self-interest, only for the safety of Israel, but voted for a vision of a nurturing society. They may have been frightened by Jesse Jackson and the Farrakhan golem he never returned to dust, and they may have felt so close to Middle America that they could hide their own history behind the prejudices of the majority. They could even enjoy looking down on the ones the others looked down on: but when it came time to pull levers, they voted with the party that put Jesse Jackson on its platform to give a speech that left the most skeptical hearts beating to the old music of brotherly love, while Old Testament Rainbows came out to witness the permanent end of the rising waters, maybe? They lost, but to be on the losing side in America is only to wait awhile and try again. In 1988 Jackson is a significant force in the Democratic party. Some Jews will desert the party. How Jews respond to the Jackson presence will affect our life in America for years to come.

Blacks too have good psychological reasons to hate Jews. They too must enjoy the release, the relief of calling other people names, of hating instead of being hated, of feeling superior to someone, of feeling that the words, dirty, criminal, destructive, antisocial, apply to someone else. Surely the anti-Semitism that is running at something of a fever pitch in the black community right now was not brought over in the holds of the slave ships, like rats from Portugal or beetles from India. It is borrowed Western terminology. It is picked up from the Holocaust, and the well-publicized Nazi positions. It is picked up from the American white culture which offered the blacks an object to hate of their very own. It must also be a balm to black pride to look with a certain pleasure—it was not us, it was them—at the history of the Jews, and while looking down on Jews and finding them morally inferior, some of the pain of the invidious comparisons between the economic and educational success of the two communities can be soothed. The fact is that blacks can join in the white majority by becoming anti-Semitic and Jews can find themselves comfortably merged with other white Americans by becoming anti-black. This path appeals to the worst instincts of both groups.

It is not a fine example of character that one group should boost its self-respect by despising another, but it is all too human and none of us are exempt from the temptation: one that occurs most often outside our conscious deliberations, in parts of the mind we cannot easily control or rationally shape.

There are many common causes that firmly unite blacks and Jews, and the passage of the sixties and its euphoric hopes has not completely undone the base of the alliance. While the strongest leaders of the black movement have come from the churches, their Christianity is of a somewhat different breed than that of white America. In many black churches the story of Jesus Christ has evolved into a liberation myth with enormous emphasis on the exodus out of

Egypt and the emphasis is less on crucifixion than on freedom, which is found in the story of the escape from slavery out from under the whips of the pharaoh. This Old Testament book remains a central part of black Christianity, and the songs of redemption, the sigh of the gospel that calls to God for refuge and justice and mercy, is the same sigh that the Jews sent out over the heaving sands at the base of Sinai.

The history of the two peoples when it avoids the, "my tragedy is worse than yours" argument is similar enough to bring together, quite naturally, with full sympathy, the hands of Heschel and Martin Luther King. For the Jews over the last two thousand years the word slavery has been primarily a metaphor for oppression, for vulnerability, for segregation, for exclusion from the universities and the paths of ownership of industry. (What else were the ghettos of Rome and Paris, of Hamburg and Budapest, but Jim Crow by another name?) Now the word slavery is used each Passover to remind us of the plight of the Jews who can not emigrate from the Soviet Union, of the forced labor and the imprisonment in the Nazi camps, places for which slavery seems too mild a word, a word of other centuries, whose intention was economic exploitation rather than genocidal destruction. But for ritual purposes, for basic meaning we all understand, slavery in Egypt has become a metaphor for all oppression, for all destruction of the people, for all peoples who are in need of divine rescue, in need of a new start, and surely none of us at the Seder table can avoid the evocation of cattle cars speeding eastward in the night. We also cannot avoid the word slavery and its resonances for blacks who only a few hundred years ago were deemed, as were the Jews, a people to whom the laws of the nations did not apply, a people more animal than human, more stuff or thing than he or she, adult or child. The call to freedom, the meaning of freedom, the mixture of God in human history, are particular to the black and Jewish combined religious and political experience. It unites us even as other matters work to sever us.

The matter of affirmative action has become the symbolic wall that is dividing the two peoples. For Jews, quotas have traditionally worked to exclude talented and justly prepared young people from entry places on the job or educational ladder. After World War II, with the conscience of the American people stunned by the pictures from Europe, anti-Semitism was exposed as the ugly beast it was, feasting on the edges of the American Dream. Quotas at the universities broke down and Jews in greater and greater numbers, numbers far larger than their proportion in the society, won places of honor and distinction, entry into the echelons of professional life. Businesses slowly but steadily hired people whose last names would have eliminated them only ten years before. Laura Hobson's *Gentleman's Agreement* became a best-seller, a famous film, and in every town with a movie house people reconsidered the issue of anti-Semitism. It served somewhat as Harriet Beecher Stowe's Uncle Tom had ninety years before, to remind America of the vision, of right and wrong. The quota system stood in the Jewish mind for prejudice, and its demise was greeted with satisfaction. Now it seems to some Jews the blacks, with the collusion of some liberals, have muddied the waters of open opportunity by attempting to legislate a way to bring back the hated quota. Of course the Jews protest. They do so in perceived self-interest. They do so because they feel about the word quota the way the blacks would feel if the Jews pressed for a return, under special circumstances, to allow, as they saw it, for correction of past injustice, segregation of toilets and water fountains in particular buildings at particular times. As people who have sorely suffered, both groups respond to hints of attack, to words that become symbols, that carry painful associations. Jewish organizations have been working behind the scenes for a kind of affirmative action, for a definition that will not frighten Jews by its numerical hardness and yet will allow for the movement upward of a people long deprived of rightful opportunity. Compromises are possible, and within the Jewish community there are important people and resources at work building bridges. The Jewish community has not allowed the political Right to sever its moral and political concerns with black issues.

With a little care and imagination we can use our reason to create coalition instead of friction. The black community needs the opportunity to win places in education and business that have been previously denied them because of race. Jews who managed to break through the same barriers without any legislated help must understand that they brought to the situation a helping hand denied blacks. Jews had an advantage: they had the right skin color, they had the right urban skills, and compensation is due the others, the ones who entered the American sweepstakes unwillingly, with handicaps forged by cruelties that Jews can all too well conjure up. If the word quota is taken out of its negative historical context, if Jews stop reacting to the concept of racial selection, as if it were other times, other situations, ones in which they were the victim, then they may realize that the word quota, like the word selection, can work for or against you, be good or bad, and that Jews cannot read into the present every echo of the past because echoes distort. If we stop promoting our own children over those of others, we can see that together we can do something for the welfare of all children.

We all know that black students do enter universities and graduate schools on their own high standing. The numbers, however, are still small, and the numbers of scholarships available for all children are shrinking. Many capable young blacks' test scores do not accurately reflect their capacities or their eventual gifts to the community. Many blacks will not need affirmative action at all, but others whose earlier education was not equal to that of the Jewish child will need an extra push. The importance of every disadvantaged black who makes it through higher education is that he or she creates a family, a new American family that stands a good chance of making our entire country stronger and healthier. They will join the ranks of blacks who are already contributing their ideas, their culture, their creativity, their individuality to the rest of us. The polls tell us now that those who make it become anti-Semitic. If it were easy to care for those of another tribe, then everyone would do it. Black anti-Semitism can be seen as a temporary illness, one that can be cured in time.

The children of parents who have obtained good educations will not need affirmative action or any other kind of special handling (another phrase with ominous connotations that is innocent in this context no matter how guilty it was in the past). Affirmative action is a stopgap, one-generation plan to correct the injustices of the past. Jews who truly care about Jewish life will break down this particular wall between black and Jew and stop gritting their teeth at the word quota and look around at the new world which requires not that we fight old battles, but that we behave with honor as we attend to the real problems still before us. What of the precedent, what if the quota system once brought back into American life is once again turned against the Jews? If the temper of the times is such that the American public wants to remove or severely limit the opportunities for Jews, as happened in Nazi Germany after 1933, then we know from hard experience that new laws will be passed, new forms of exclusion will be created: absolutely no precedent is necessary, nothing beyond a storm of reawakened anti-Semitism will be required, and while this is always a realistic possibility and we forget it at our peril, we cannot stave it off by overreactions in the present, reactions that dim our light unto the nations.

But back to those polls that tell us how middle-class blacks feel today about Jews—why should Jews be concerned about the numbers of blacks in graduate schools when those very blacks are the ones expressing the most virulent anti-Semitic sentiments? Is a pro-affirmative-action position simply a new twist of Jewish liberal masochism? There are those who believe so but there are others working for a real reconciliation. Jesse Jackson has stated that Mr. Farrakhan's anti-Semitic remarks are "reprehensible and morally indefensible." He has said that "Blacks and Jews are bound by shared blood and shared sacrifices." He has said that he "condemns Israel's action in selling arms to South Africa but not the State of Israel and its need to exist." This is a position many Jews both in Israel and in the Diaspora would agree with. Israel in fact passed a law after a difficult debate in the Knesset forbidding exactly such martial trade. Whether Jews can trust Jesse Jackson or not seems an irrelevant question. Whether one likes him or not is even more irrelevant. He is not focused on Jewish interests. He is not a supporter of Israel right or wrong and he may or may not be to some extent anti-Semitic. We do not have to vote for him but his influence in the Democratic party will hardly lead to an abandonment of Israel or an outbreak of anti-Semitic legislation in this country. We can begin the process of understanding. Why do blacks admire him? How did he become their leader and what can Jews do to reach over Farrakhan's head and begin real conversation with the black community? We may have to talk with Jesse Jackson for a while because he is their most visible leader. No need to be fooled into naive admiration of Jackson and no need to go off into a hysterical anti-Jackson position. Caution, respect for black pride, will be more effective in the long run. The current anti-Semitism among educated blacks, when it is seen as a mean-spirited crutch for crippled self-respect, can be reversed. This year's bad temper can have passed by the time the polls of 1990 are taken. Perhaps history need not mindlessly repeat itself and the blacks need not be the enemy of the Jew. They do not have to become like the peasants of the Ukraine, some of whom joined the Nazis, or the workers of Warsaw, some of whom turned their back on Jews. Perhaps this time we can break the vicious cycle that has always pitted the groups at the bottom of the social order against each other. The Muse of History gives us warnings, it does not do crystal-ball readings.

Jesse Jackson represents to the blacks of America what David Ben-Gurion and Golda Meir represented to the young Israel. Jesse Jackson holds for blacks the same kind of symbolic power that Franklin Roosevelt held for poor Americans, that William Jennings Bryan held for farmers and country people. We must maximize his offers of friendship and take whatever help he may offer, for whatever political reasons of his own, to bring the Jewish and the black world closer. We may not now need an alliance with blacks in order to protect our interests in America—that is true enough—but we do need such an alliance in order to preserve our sense of Jewish morality, Jewish faith, Jewish identity.

But what of the well-known pro–Palestine Liberation Organization position of the educated black? What can this mean except permanent tension between Jews committed to the safety and survival of Israel and blacks who have joined in the chorus that chants Zionism is racism into the world's ear? This linkage of Zionism and racism is a pernicious but wildly successful propaganda piece launched by the Soviets on the part of the Arab world. First it satisfies all those who were feeling uncomfortable because the Jews held the moral high ground after the Holocaust. See, this slogan says, Jews are just as bad as Nazis, which means that now we have wiped the moral slate clean and no one owes the Jews anything. They were bad people all along. Then it makes automatic allies of the black countries with the Palestinians who allegedly suffer as the blacks did because they are not white, European, descendants of the imperialists. The genius of this slogan is that it gives the blacks someone else to hate, to blame, to organize against, and how convenient it is that this new enemy, the Zionist, distracts attention from the real racism on Main Street, U.S.A. The blacks can identify with the PLO's Yasir Arafat, gunman extraordinaire, terrorist, and statesman, a victim of history like themselves, but unlike themselves, a victim who carries a gun, has an army, ragtaggle or not, and is taken to lunch by heads of state the world over.

It is hard to fight a slogan, especially one that is not based in reality. It is hard to cut through the romance of the PLO with the real history and the real facts of the embattled territory that is both Palestine and Israel. It is hard to tell the story of the Balfour Declaration, the Arab riots in 1929, the Arab rejection of partition in 1948, the refusal of the Arab countries to resettle the refugees who have spent two generations in camps. It is hard now to fairly and calmly trace the Jewish claim to the land, the blood on the hands of Arab intransigence as well as the aggression that now has a Jewish name.

Like other Americans, the Jew of the 1980s is not so idealistic as the Jew of the 1930s. The Jew of the 1980s has no faith in universal promises and an enormous reserve of anger that needs to be spent, that can be spent on the heads of blacks without too much immediate political or social danger. The blacks are moving forward, at least in their political awakening, and with that they have discovered deep wells of anger that rush forth and spill over onto the Jews.

The author Jerzy Kosinski wrote in *The Painted Bird,* "A person [concludes the boy] should take revenge for every wrong or humiliation. There were far too many injustices in the world to have them all weighed and judged. A man should consider every wrong he had suffered and decide on the appropriate revenge. Only the conviction that one was as strong as the enemy and that one could pay him back double, enabled people to survive." This bitter view is reasonable enough for a Jew who knows his history. It is reasonable for a black. This pulling in of lines, me against them, mine against theirs, is a legitimate if dangerous Holocaust response. However, the Holocaust showed us all the cataclysm that occurs when one group is mythologized into the demon, the scapegoat, the subhuman. It demonstrated the absolute evil in bigotry and the catastrophic results of dehumanizing human life. Jew hatred in Europe is not unlike black hatred in South Boston, in the Klan rallies of

South Carolina, in the rhetoric of the Aryan Nations. We know after the Holocaust that if we fight racism against one group, we are fighting a state of mind, an attitude natural to man and very contagious, a propensity to despise, a joy in hatred, a universal capacity for banding together and hunting another, a capacity that could turn on us, that history has demonstrated will turn on us in time. Jews know that first they come for Jews and then they come for you. This can easily be read, first they do to blacks and then they do to you. Blacks should understand this: even if they come for the Jews, that does not prevent them from coming another time for the blacks. The recurrent virus of personal hatred must be vanquished before any of us can feel permanently safe in this society. Paradoxically enough (another paradox), the Holocaust teaches Jewish self-interest at the very same time that it confirms that Jewish interests require the breaking down of barriers between peoples, the necessity of widening the total human capacity for empathy. It teaches black self-interest at the very moment it shows the necessity for human empathy with all peoples. Tribal loyalty is a sword that cuts the hand that wields it.

So we fight black anti-Semitism the same way we fight any other kind of anti-Semitism, not by turning on innocent children who need school lunches or by abandoning any of our traditional Jewish commandments to care for the stranger, to care for the poor, to protect the sick, to make the world a better place. As we attend the nastiness of bigotry no matter its object, we remove poison gas from our air, the same air we all breathe. Imagine 200,000 blacks from suburbs and inner cities massed on Washington, voices raised and placards held high to protest the imprisonment of Soviet Jews. Imagine 200,000 Jews, with heads covered and heads bare, from Williamsburg and Shaker Heights, gathered in front of the South African embassy to protest apartheid. Ah, that will be the day, you say. Yes, that will be the day: the beginning of the end of multiple tribes and multiple peoples.

The Holocaust has left us angry and even if we take care our anger may get misplaced on the heads of innocent bystanders, where it will perpetuate divisions that are not only cruel and indecent but may also work against everyone's safety in the long run. We can answer the paradox of the Holocaust: universal vs. particular in such a way that we, black and Jew, watching out for our own interests, can still consider the imperatives of our bond to all others. In that process we may heal the divisions of tribes, the divisions that lead to blaming the lack of progress of some black children on the heads of Jewish teachers and the blaming of blacks for all the diseases of urban life. Survival does not depend as Kosinski's character would have it on retaliation, revenge, warfare. It rests on our friendships, on our ending the cycles of destruction. The name-calling can stop, and having seen in the Holocaust the shape of the end, we can take warning and turn toward each other, or we can turn on each other in an orgy of self-protection that will leave us, once again beasts, gnawing on bones.

Poles and Jews

THORNS IN THE SIDE

The ambiguous nature of Polish action during World War II is still an issue that arouses intense feeling on all sides. We need to understand the Polish response to Hitler almost as much as we need to understand Hitler himself. The Nazis behaved as if possessed by demons, as if Evil itself was walking among us. The Poles behaved like people, ordinary people. Those demons are gone for the moment. The ordinary people remain. This makes them the focus of our Holocaust questions.

This drama between Jew and non-Jew takes place all over Europe but in Poland it gathers an intensity, a horror, that rivets attention as if one were watching a person who had clasped left and right hand together and no matter how he struggled could not untangle his fingers, releasing the grip. It is as if the two peoples, small and singular, holding on to identity despite the crushing political realities, both frequently at the trigger point of the Western world's anger, both comparatively weak and yet persistent, became through no choice of their own leading actors in some passion play that seems to have epilogue after epilogue long after the final curtain has gone down. It is as if Nazi Germany became a calamity, like a hurricane or an earthquake, against which the human actors with real human frailties could play out their fates and explore the moral questions of their time.

There were three and one-half million Jews living in Poland in 1939, more than in any other nation. Almost all of those who did not leave in time were killed. Some few survived, hidden with false papers among the Christians; some were kept in barns and cellars and attics by Christians who risked their lives and the lives of their families. But many were betrayed. The Jewish world, a world of assimilated Jews walking the streets of Warsaw practicing professions such as science and medicine, is now gone. The world of religious Jews, whole villages and towns of Jews who wore black coats and whose wives and daughters lit the candles on Friday night have vanished as if they were never there, as if those communities, their fiddlers on the roof, their mikvahs and shuls, their cheders and prayer books, were simply shadows and a shift of light wiped them away. The Poles moved into the emptied Jewish houses and the ghetto of Warsaw was built upon like the seventh city of Troy. The famous Yeshiva of Lublin is now a medical clinic. The Jewish graveyards are abandoned and the stones have fallen among the weeds. The synagogues that were not burned to the ground have been turned into stables, warehouses, government offices. Today Jewish life exists only in photographs, in imagination, in memory.

Is Poland worrying that its Jews won't stay in the graveyard? Is that why the government in the midst of social unrest in the early days of Solidarity, the workers protest movement, began an anti-Semitic campaign against the Jews who were no longer there?

The Polish-Jewish question has become the path that some have taken to understand and interpret the Holocaust. William Styron, who wanted to argue the universal horror of the Holocaust and play down its Jewish nature, chose a Polish heroine to suffer the Nazi crime. When Claude Lanzmann was looking for a way to explain the Holocaust, he found himself talking to Poles in little villages, to Poles who watched the trains go by. When the German officials were planning the Final Solution, did they place their camps in Poland because of the distance from the civilized capitals of Europe, because of the large concentration of Jews in Poland, and perhaps because they knew that the Poles as a group would not object to their plans? The major Jewish resistance took place in Warsaw. The Jews remember Warsaw as the Masada of Europe. The city of Warsaw is always in flames on the Jewish map.

When the argument is made that the Holocaust did not just happen to Jews, the fate of the Polish intelligentsia is raised and the Polish resistance and the Polish children who were stolen for breeding purposes in Germany are mourned. A Polish priest has been canonized for allowing himself to be killed in the place of another Polish Catholic. No Italian, French, Belgian, German priest, was found behaving like a saint in Auschwitz. But many other Polish priests never let an Easter pass without telling their people that the Jews had killed Christ. The canonized priest himself was the editor of a virulently anti-Semitic newspaper in the days before the invasion. Poles were victims and they were Jewish protectors and they were also Jewish betrayers, some by indifference, others by direct intention. Poland was occupied by a brutal and ruthless conqueror. The Poles were neither respected nor rewarded by German occupation. They would have been slaughtered in great numbers had their resistance been stronger. They, unlike the Danes, had no escape route by sea for their Jews. Unlike the Danes, they had a clear picture of German ferocity and the necessity for submission for the sake of survival. Out of the historical context, out of the time itself, it is simply obscene for anyone of us to judge, to estimate our own response, to take the imaginary temperature of our own altruism under the threat of death. Nevertheless, we cannot help but wonder if the fate of the Jews of Eastern Europe might have been different had the Poles with one voice protested as the Danes did, if they had mounted massive attacks on the camps, if they had just sabotaged a few of the train tracks headed toward Sobibor, Treblinka, Auschwitz. If the Poles had resisted the extermination of their Jews with the same courage that they now seem to face government interference with their churches, their labor unions, well, then, more Jews would have lived, and although more Poles would certainly have died (is it moral for Jews to have wished this, to have required it?), the Poles and the Jews might now be able to look at each other across history without those echoes of shame, blame, justification.

Historians say that it was not possible given the conditions of the time for the Poles to have acted against the Final Solution. Their armies were overrun. Their resistance small and easily betrayed. But historians have only facts at their disposal and Jews, out of their grief, and their knowledge of the sad tale of Polish anti-Semitism, its pogroms and its libels, will go on wondering if greater resistance might not have changed the facts, altered the conditions. Wondering is not passing judgment on the actions of each and every Pole. Those who wonder if the Poles might have done better cannot assume their own behavior would have been exemplary under the Nazi gun. But we can no more stop this wondering because logic tells us it has no point than we can stop mourning because mourning does not bring back the dead.

The drama of collaboration or resistance, heroism at grave risk, or silent acquiescence, is a European question. It occurred in every country the Nazis entered. The same events took place in France, in Belgium, in Holland, in Italy, in the Scandinavian countries, in Hungary, Romania, Greece, and Yugoslavia, and each country reacted a little differently based on the number of Jews in their midst, the government in power, the traditions of the people, the degree of assimilation of their Jews; but the Poles, despite the numbers of righteous Gentiles among them, have come to represent the collaboration of the Christians in the mass murder of Jews because the Jews were killed on their land, because they had such a vivid history of anti-Semitism prior to the invasion, because Poland, since the Jews had been invited to settle in the fourteenth century, had become the center of Jewish civilization in the Diaspora.

In 1987 the Catholic independent weekly newspaper, *Tygodnik Powszechny,* published an article on Polish anti-Semitism that began a major debate. The piece by Jan Blonski, a well-known literary critic, said, "To clean Cain's field, we must remember Abel. He lived in our house, on our soil, his blood has sunk into the soil whether we want it or not. It has penetrated our memory and ourselves. Thus we must purify ourselves by seeing ourselves truly. Without that, the houses, the soil, and ourselves shall remain branded." He was struggling with the question of Polish character. Are Poles more callous, more likely than peoples of other nations to turn their back on human pain? The debate is on among Poles. Such thinking presents a clear trap for Jews. If Poles can be thought of as more brutal than others, then Jews can be thought of as more venal, shrewder, and so on with the list of stereotypes that divide and destroy. If Jews attribute peculiar undesirable characteristics to one nation, we have entered the business of denigration of whole peoples, a position the Holocaust has taught can lead to flames. The tarring of any nation with a wide brush is something Jews might sensibly avoid. The debate that began with Blonski has naturally evoked a strong response. The newspaper received hundreds of letters, most of them highly anti-Semitic. Wadyslav Sila Howicki, a seventy-four-year-old lawyer, a member of the Polish resistance, wrote to the paper in a fury: "What could we do—attack the camps with the forces we had—to suffer enormous losses and doom all those in the camps? Let no man lecture us about unfulfilled duties, and let no Mr. Blonski say that we came close to the crime of genocide." This is an understandable protest from a man who fought and risked his own life against the invader and who remembers himself as a hero in harsh times; but wait, Mr. Sila Howicki cannot leave it at that, he goes on to say, "The passivity of the Jews and their submission to German orders was the first and basic impediment preventing our giving greater help to the Jews." Ah, he blames the Jews for their fate. It is not that Poles were lacking in morality: Jews were weak and compliant. This remark might indicate an uneasy conscience. He goes too far to justify himself. Why must he blame the victim? Perhaps because he knows that Poles did not behave altogether well: that the Polish resistance refused to send arms to the ghetto fighters when they begged for them, that Jews escaping into the woods to join partisan groups would sometimes be welcomed and sometimes be shot. He wrote his letter, he raised his voice, because he is not completely confident that the decisions taken in those hot times were the ethically correct, the tactically correct decisions. Forty some years have gone by and he has tried to bury the memory of the Poles of the working-class neighborhood who had often beaten Jews who had wandered into their streets. He has forgotten the vast number of anti-Semitic publications and pamphlets on Polish newsstands in the 1930s that were as common then as are lottery tickets today. He has ignored the Polish right-wing party which had called for Jewish elimination from the universities long before the Nazi planes flew overhead. He has forgotten the Poles who later waited at the edges of the ghetto to catch the Jews who had escaped through sewers, hoping to lose their already lost selves among the throngs of Warsaw.

Jews tell stories, terrible stories of Polish colleagues who gave them away in order to possess their apartments, their jewelry. Jews tell stories of begging for help and being turned away with starving children in their arms, with elderly parents begging by their side. Jews on the whole do not have a warm feeling toward Poles, who in fact still speak, and we hear it in the Lanzmann film *Shoah,* we hear it in the voice of the official government functionaries, of Jewish money, of Jewish women who are lazy and rich and steal the men of deserving Polish girls, of Jews who hid their gold, money that they had taken from the good Catholics of Poland, in pots behind their stoves. We hear it in the words of devout believers who speak as their priests have spoken for centuries of Jews as Christ killers, a people deserving of punishment because of what they did to the beloved Savior.

Polish Jewish survivors on the whole do not feel safe with Poles, and when the Solidarity movement rose against the Stalinist state, many Jews had mixed feelings as they watched the evening news report on the hero Lech Walesa and the proud, independent freedom-seeking workers of Poland. They were moved by the cause, but not by the people. They remembered Poles who had cheered as their former neighbors marched through the streets on their way to deportation and Poles who had thrown them out of the university, out of their jobs at newspapers, banks, medical clinics. For the Jews the Pole has grown to represent the brutal anti-Semite, whose landscape contained the death camps, whose people carried on with their lives, rode, as Czeslaw Milosz wrote in his poem, "Campo Di Fiori," on the merry-go-round outside the ghetto walls as Jews were placed on lists with eastern destinations.

In 1946, on the fourth day of July, the townspeople of Kielce murdered the entire group of forty-two Jews who had made their way back to the town after the camps were liberated. They did this despite the fact that there were no Germans to cheer them on. One might have expected that they would welcome the Jews who had survived such terror and help them rebuild their businesses and homes. But they didn't want Jews in Kielce. When word of the massacre spread through Eastern Europe, many other Jews recognized the futility of trying to return and went on to Palestine, to America, to South America. Poland is the only country in Europe where Jews returning after the war's end were murdered. One Jewish woman, a refugee from Lublin, whose whole family was gone, who had left for America in 1938, speaking in her New York apartment as we watched a television documentary on modern-day Poland, said, "I don't care if they have to wait in line for butter and eggs. We waited in line for trains and ovens. Let them eat air." That the Poles we were watching on the television set were different human beings than the ones who had shrugged as her parents and brothers and sisters were lined up in the square made no difference to her. Just as the seventy-four-year-old leader of the Polish resistance could find no guilt in his nation, so she could find no forgiveness in her heart.

Members of the Polish underground, wanting to be recognized as the Polish army, the representatives of the Polish people, nearly did themselves in with erratic gestures of comic-opera bravado by attacking the vastly stronger German army as the Russians waited at the borders of Poland. But these same brave partisans, ready to face death for the honor of their country, did not lose any unnecessary men in forays into the ghetto, into the camps, onto the train tracks. One lost cause was noble, the other just a lost cause.

But that is only part of the story and the rue that runs through the Jewish community when one speaks of Poles has an antidote in the stories that are also told, of Polish neighbors who took a child, who claimed an old mother as their own, who hid and fed, and deceived for Jewish families, out of decency, out of compassion, out of horror at the Nazi exterminations. We know of Polish men and women who were shot or hanged or starved in camps because of attempts to save Jews. Poles did go to concentration camps because they had hidden Jews. Poles behaved with great heroism and altruism and many are recognized among the Path for Righteous Gentiles that lies in Yad Vashem in Israel. The truth, forty years later, is becoming somewhat clearer. The Poles were frequently anti-Semitic. They lived beside and with Jewish communities that were very different from them, that remained merchants and tradespeople while many of the Poles worked with their hands, worked the land. The resentments were ancient. All the causes of anti-Semitism, magical, mythical, and economic and political were embedded deep in the Polish mind.

The Poles lived with their Jews the way the white southerners lived with their blacks, only in this case the fortunes of both groups were fragile and life was hard enough for everyone. The Jews appeared as Internationalists, not supporters of the state, and so angered the Rightists, the Nationalists. But politics was an additional excuse for a suspicion so deep rooted and pervasive that it held the entire Jewish community, man, woman, and child, at fault for the ideologies of a few. After the Second World War anti-Semitism revived with an attack on those Jews who had returned to Poland and became officials in the Communist party. When the people wished to vent spleen on the Communists, they expressed hatred of the Jews, who after all were in this case no different from any other Communist and could not reasonably be hated as Jews, but as Communists, and this could once again not reasonably have applied to every man, woman, and child of Jewish origin. Anti-Semitism has been used since the seventeenth century by the Polish peasantry in their anger against the authorities, whoever they might be, and it has been used by the government, the feudal powers, to divert attention from other real grievances. The Jews from their first arrival on the Polish border have appeared to be aligned with the power of the state. Polish hatred falls on the heads of Jews whether they speak for revolution or for the established order.

The Jew has become for some Poles a kind of totem of rottenness. If they can blame enough on the Jews, they hope to cleanse themselves. It can easily be understood that Jews would find in the history of anti-Semitism in Poland a line of development that led inevitably to the catastrophic events of the Hitler era.

The argument is made that Poles cannot be blamed for the things that happened to Jews because Poles themselves were the target of Nazi cruelty. The two groups were co-sufferers at the hands of a vicious invader. This argument for equal time on some catastrophe scale does not ring with conviction, no matter how many monuments dot the countryside with that legend engraved at the base. Poles were killed by Nazis for all kinds of crossing of the totalitarian regime's lines. They too suffered incredible losses at the hands of the Nazis, but they were not killed simply because of who they were, because of their birth certificate, because of their grandparents. They had a chance to walk through the streets without being murdered, to go to work, to shop for food, to bear children, to make love: life was not normal but it was possible to gather fuel, to pick a flower, to continue. Poles who were interned in the camps were given finite sentences and were allowed to keep their own clothes. They were not subject to automatic selection for the gas chambers. The Polish suffering was not equivalent to the Jewish disaster and equating the two is an attempt to change history, to mock history, to divert us from the peculiar fate of the Jews in Europe and to confuse our understanding of man's monster face, the face he carries right under the mask of civilization.

The Poles have on their conscience not the camps or the trenches outside of Lublin and Lvov but the atmosphere of bigotry, emanating openly from the pulpit and the classroom, the libels against Jews that involved money, the special quality of Jew hatred that had been nourished in the particular crucible of Polish society, of aristocrats and peasantry, of semi-feudal land arrangements, and deep religiosity that could and did light up murderous passions. This anti-Semitism had pervaded Poland long before the Nazis came and naturally enough increased its tempo with the permission and encouragement of the Nazi conqueror. The vast propaganda machine of the Nazi state, its newspapers, posters, radio programs, created an environment that gave encouragement to and fanned the anti-Semitism that Poland could claim as its very own.

But the Poles and the Jews also have many things in common. It can be said that the Poles were the Jews of Western Europe. The status of the Slavs was only a few notches higher than that of the Jews in the Nazi hierarchy of race. The Poles have had to maintain identity and language against conquering armies, alien governments for centuries. The Poles on the eastern edge of Europe were not counted among the great civilized nations of Christendom. Years after the war, when anti-Semitism was no longer openly fashionable, when its consequences too grim for casual humor, we saw the arrival across the Western world of the Polish joke, many of those stories a direct steal on the Fools of Chelm stories that Jews told on themselves. Were these jokes started by Jews? Probably not. They existed in Eastern Europe before the war and were part of every Czechoslovakian schoolboy's repertoire, but the postwar spread of these jokes, the wide distance the wave of Polish jokes now traveled, seems to signal a mutation of anti-Semitism that emphasizes the kinship between the Pole and the Jew. It tells us that mockery of another people, a foretaste of hatred, seems to be endemic in the human condition and needs outlets official or otherwise. The Polish joke, with its steady emphasis on Polish stupidity, provides the world with just such a vent: harmless enough in itself but not so clean in its origin. It is true that Jews in the privacy of their houses have for centuries taken revenge on the anti-Semitism of their neighbors by portraying them as dumb. Jews have long thought of Poles as less intelligent. With this counterprejudice, this comforting illusion of having something of value the other did not, Jews consoled themselves, comforted themselves through the centuries of physical and social abuse. The accusation of dullness seems to have risen from the cauldron of Polish-Jewish bigotry and on wings of the dead, spread across the seas and turned into a contempt for Poles, who now became stand-ins for the original object of hate.

The Poles are not easily rid of their Jewish past. When the Polish pope goes to Auschwitz to honor the dead, he must go to Poland. When Israeli heads of state, when leaders of the Jewish community, make pilgrimages to the camps, they must go to Poland, and the land of Poland and people of Poland will forever be implicated in the Holocaust. When the leaders of Solidarity catch the attention of the world in their pleas for freedom, for a more open society, we see the stirrings of life from beneath a shroud, but the shroud is still there.

The matter is not a simple one. The closer one looks, the more the Polish villain disappears into the crowd. Once the Nazi program had begun in Poland, many Poles acquiesced because they had no more choice than the Jews who packed their belongings and gathered in public squares. The Poles will go on defending their behavior during the war, and from the outside from the distance of forty-odd years, it seems that no clear judgment can be made. Certainly we cannot judge an entire populace on either the acts of kindness or the acts of cruelty of a few. This is not to say that the atmosphere of anti-Semitism, the underlying hatred that surely characterized much of Polish life, did not serve as a silencer, as an accomplice to the act, as a kind of release for the Polish people who had lost their nation and their pride, but could still feel superior to Jews who were going to lose life itself. Today Jews cannot meet Poles without suspicion, without believing that they are complicit in genocide, and the Holocaust hangs over both groups, a deadly weight, an undigested stone, a hindrance to the tasks at hand, a reminder of guilt, a guilt that only foments more anger while spinning itself in useless circles.

In another seventy-five years the Jewish settlements in Poland will be forgotten completely except by the Jews who will remember but will no longer weep, so what can we learn now from the Polish-Jewish connection? First, perhaps, we see the scene in Poland in 1939–1945 as evidence, additional evidence of the fact that human societies are irredeemably tribal, familial and hostile to outsiders, and that words of brotherhood, tolerance, religious respect, are flimsy concepts that fall by the wayside in the daily living of men and women of different cultures.

The Polish-Jewish question lingers in our minds, takes up many pages in *The New York Review of Books,* becomes the center of the arguments about Lanzmann's *Shoah,* because it functions like a ghost limb, it suffers pain after amputation. It is kind of a reverse lesson, a cautionary tale. The subject was discussed at the Oxford conference in September 1985, by writers and historians from Poland and Israel. The meeting produced an Institute for Polish-Jewish Studies and a yearbook called *Polin*. In the winter of 1988 the Polish government announced an apology to the Jews who were thrown out of the Communist party in the purges after the war. It has promised to support the work of the Institute for Polish-Jewish Studies. This is a promising beginning, and these steps may open the path for real mutual understanding and reconciliation.

The subject, far from losing power as we grow distant from the events, seems to gain in fascination, in importance. More conferences are planned. More publications will be issued, translated into many languages. The Pole is Everyman. The Jew is the victim. The victim is angry with Everyman who watched his execution. Everyman is angry with the Jew because he dares to make him feel guilty, to reproach him with acts of less than heroic dimension. Everyman cannot apologize because that would be to admit an intolerable and unreasonable burden of guilt. The Jew cannot help but insist on that apology or at least a recognition of what he believes occurred. The Jew cannot help but insist on that apology, cannot stop himself from demanding it: he owes it to the dead, he needs the apology to put his pain to rest. He is made angry by Everyman's attempt to forget, to bypass the issue, to include himself in the suffering. Everyman is angry with the Jew who would deny him honor, who hurts nationalistic pride, who makes the good Catholic who confessed and prayed and went to Mass every Sunday feel tainted, as if original sin was of more recent times. It is certain that causing people to feel guilty, especially about a horror in which they may barely have participated, have only heard of from parents or grandparents, may not remember, may not have been a part of at all, is fruitless. On the other hand, insisting on how bad things were for you during the war, how hard it was to be Polish when the Nazis came, how unimportant and outside your ken was the Jewish disaster, will not work either. There will always be some Jew to insist that the inscription on the monument to Nazi brutality and Polish suffering should have included him, that it didn't happen entirely behind Polish backs, that synagogue fires were in fact lit by the Polish police.

Lucjan Dobroszycki, the Jewish historian who has written the definitive record of the Lodz ghetto, says, "I must put aside bitterness as I work. I must be objective and rational." It is to the credit of the human mind that bitterness can be put aside and human actions placed in historical context and the other side, the full side, the forces of politics, geography, fortune, can all be observed and the events of the Holocaust recorded as accurately as possible for the generations to come. Only in this way will we ever see the portrait of the human face in the mirror of our deeds. For the rest of us who are not historians, both Jews and Poles, we too had best hold our bitterness to one side and extend our capacities to understand, and feel for the other. First we need the truth that only the historians and witnesses can supply, and then if Pole and Jew reach toward each other, someday we may heal this festering.

Of course in time feelings will die along with the participants, victims and witnesses, the ones who were moved out of apartments and the ones who moved in. But the memory will remain. Jews will be in Poland as an invisible force, as a voice of conscience for many generations to come. Poland will be in Jews wherever they are and not just in their Hasidic communities which have hardly changed their dress since the eighteenth century, but in all of us who will pull a vanished Poland along wherever we go. May the decent memories return in time. May we find a way to move the argument away from who did what, who suffered the most, who is entitled to pity and who to scorn, because this argument will only go round in circles till we are all silenced by exhaustion. Eventually we will have to leave it to time. Let it go. Before the end of the twenty-first century there will surely be enough human suffering to go around, and there may even be enough goodness about so that we can all take pride in our nations. Or perhaps there will be no nations, our tribalism will have murdered us all, in which event this Polish-Jewish question will float like all the other unanswered conflicts toward the stars.

Jews and Catholics

A TRADITION DIVIDED

There is an old joke told by Jews in America of a horrid rotten apple of a Jewish boy, who wouldn't do his homework, sassed the teacher, tortured the girls, and got report cards that made his mother sick. Desperate, his parents enrolled him in the local Catholic school hoping for a better result. The first report card came back, all A's and an A+ in deportment. "What happened?" asked the delighted father. "All over the school," said the son, "they got pictures of a guy on a cross. That's what they do if a Jewish kid doesn't behave." The relationship between Catholic and Jew has been full of misunderstanding at its best and violence at its worst.

The Catholic Church has long held the Jewish community in its hands. Sometimes it has protected the Jews, sometimes it has not. By not accepting Christ as the Messiah, the Jews put themselves in the position of heretics, a great variety of whom were burned off the face of the globe in the first ten centuries C.E. as the Church consolidated its power and its dogma. But the Jews had a special relationship with the Catholics. The Old Testament was included in the Holy Writ, a status formalized in the Code of Theodosius in 438 C.E. Yosef Yerushalmi explains in a paper delivered at a conference at the Episcopal Cathedral of Saint John the Divine in New York City that if the Old Testament were to be considered of value, then the Jews themselves, as representatives, carriers of the baggage of the past, as speakers of Hebrew, a holy language, as pilgrims partially on the way, were themselves deserving of some care. At least this was the official position, and while the populace of the towns and the villages of Europe may have turned against their Jews from time to time, the bishops and the cardinals, the higher officials of the Vatican, tended to protect the Jews, to insist that they not be murdered in the streets. This is not to say that inside the Vatican they admired Jews. Their position was that the Jews had always rejected the Prophets and refused to hear their message of repentance just as they turned away from the words of Jesus. The Catholic scholar Rosemary Radford Ruether reports at the conference that circumcision came to be interpreted by Christian theologians as the mark of Cain by which Jews are to be preserved to the end of time as a wandering reprobate people. She goes on to say that "Christian Theology demanded Jewish existence although in a state of reprobation, as the continuing witness to the triumph of the Church and as the final witness to Christ at the end of time." This attitude toward the Jews, while not as benign as it might have been had the words of Jesus been taken as seriously as the miracles that attended his life and death, did save Jews a place in the hierarchy of medieval Europe and allowed them to survive even under adverse conditions. It also conveniently provided a group that could lend and circulate money, a service that was badly needed in the economy of the preindustrial Europe. As Sabbath goys performed necessary tasks for religious communities of Jews, so even more crucially did banker Jews supply money for enterprises and expansion. The moneylender was considered immoral and naturally enough hated by his debtors. The role was perilous at best but certainly tolerated and utilized by the Church.

So while the Gnostics and others with unusual or nonconforming religious ideas perished, the Jews survived. The official Catholic Church did not encourage or participate in any forms of violent anti-Semitism. It is nevertheless true that individual parish priests in all Catholic countries, during the centuries, looking for examples of deviltry, of betrayal, of ways to dramatize the morality of Jesus, did enflame their congregants, did add to the burden of Jewish life, did increase the dangers of helpless communities whose members could be accused of causing a plague, a shortage of rain, of making ritual objects from the blood of Christian children. The Catholic position that Jews killed the Savior clearly made a beachhead from which attacks on Jews could be launched seasonally like other celebrations.

The small assaults that occurred regularly in every town in Europe in which Jews had been allowed to settle were dwarfed by the hysteria of the Crusades in which the messianic validity of Jesus Christ was to be forced upon reluctant communities, who were sometimes murdered en masse: men, women, children screaming while soldiers did what they believed was God's work.

All this was prelude, a background for the Nazi times. The Vatican under Pope Pius XI did issue a statement condemning the Nuremberg Laws in 1936. The pope then wanted to put forth another encyclical in 1938 when he learned of Kristallnacht. He asked his two assistants to prepare memoranda to help formulate his thoughts. One of his assistants, Angelo Cardinal Roncalli, prepared a strong condemnation of the events of that brutal night. The other, Eugenio Cardinal Pacelli, former nuncio in Germany, and in 1938 the secretary of state to the Holy See, counseled that the Vatican be silent because he believed that Hitler was the only barrier between the West and the atheist menace from the East. The pope died before he could decide between the opposing views of his assistants. His successor was Pacelli, who became Pope Pius XII. His role in the Nazi-Jewish drama has been subjected to a good deal of scrutiny with an ambiguous conclusion. He protected the Jews of Rome and may have interceded with the Nazis on several occasions to slow or halt deportations, but he did not publicly confront or condemn anti-Semitism. The times demanded a moral hero, and it seems that Pope Pius XII was more of a statesman than a crusader. In a famous photograph we see a line of Austrian bishops greeting the German troops as they march into Vienna with their arms outstretched in the Hitler salute.

On the other hand, Cardinal Pietro of Rome helped thousands of Italian Jews, hiding, providing funds, arranging networks of safe places. Many parish priests did their best to protect children, taking the endangered people into monasteries and convents. But others advised their parishioners to cooperate with the Nazi authorities. The pope is not considered infallible on worldly political matters, but his leadership is crucial to the direction and the tone of the entire Church. The Vatican could have denounced the anti-Semitism of the Nazis, the ghettoization of all Jews, the deportations, as morally wrong, as anti-Christian. The Vatican was silent because it was concerned about the welfare of Catholics in countries under Nazi control, including German Catholics and Polish Catholics. The Vatican was silent because the Germans were thought to be heading off the godless Russians, the Bolshevik menace, whose hostility to religion opposed Church authority. The Vatican urged

Catholic members of the German Parliament to vote for Hitler in the election of 1933, because of its conviction that he was the man to stop the Communists. In the 1940s Catholics were excommunicated for advocating divorce or abortion, but Hitler, himself a Catholic, was never excommunicated by his Church despite his policies of euthanasia, extermination, and conquest.

The Vatican revealed its insensitivity to the Jewish plight when at the war's end when no political agenda would be advanced by placating or cooperating with the Nazis, after the tragedy of the camps had become clear to every living person, the Vatican helped Nazi war criminals escape, hiding them in the Vatican halls, providing passports to Catholic countries in South America where no one would care how many Jews were gone and who was responsible.

When Cardinal Roncalli, after returning from Turkey where his old political adversary, Cardinal Pacelli, had sent him, became Pope John XXIII, he released to the world the memos he and Cardinal Pacelli had written to the pope in 1938, revealing the Vatican's inner discussions of the Jewish issue. In 1963, the Vatican issued a new encyclical that altered its long-held official position toward the Jews, saying that Jews should not be considered the killers of Christ. Statements were made about building friendships, increasing contacts, sharing scholars, forming new committees to study texts and problematic areas between the two religions. This was possible in Vatican politics, not only because of the leadership of Pope John XXIII but because of the Holocaust. The Holocaust making a demand on the conscience of the Catholic hierarchy, the Holocaust making clear that the concept of punishing the Jew because he had not accepted Jesus, because he had committed deicide, had itself become an anti-Christian factor. The facts of the Holocaust made the accusation of Jewish deicide unpalatable. When the punishment of the Jews went to such an extreme, the idea of a loving and merciful God was itself threatened. Although it took many years before the Vatican could come out with a clear statement that the concept of Jewish deicide was wrong, the spreading knowledge of the Holocaust began the ongoing dialogues that have, despite continued tensions, brought Jew and Catholic closer together, closer than ever before.

The next chapter in Jewish-Catholic relations should have been one of increased tolerance, mutual sharing of scholarly resources, and a general atmosphere of religious tolerance that would show the world how it goes when civilization works. We are not yet there. Frictions and tensions keep rising, and the memory of the Holocaust, as well as bringing the two religions closer, keeps creating new irritations, new frustrations, and some are quite serious.

There is the peculiar matter of Edith Stein and the Carmelite nunnery planned for the edges of Auschwitz, a place where the good nuns could offer prayers for the souls of the murdered ones, prayers presumably more effective because they were conceived at the murder site itself. Edith Stein was a Jewish intellectual philosopher who converted to Catholicism and ultimately joined the Carmelite order while continuing to write philosophical tracts on her religious convictions. In August of 1942 she and her sister, also a convert but of no known intellectual distinction, were taken from their convent in Holland where they had sought refuge and sent to Auschwitz where they perished on arrival. Pope John Paul II has beatified Edith Stein so now she is on the way toward sainthood. While from the Catholic point of view this is a great honor, it troubles the Jewish community because she didn't die as a Catholic martyr. She died because she was an ordinary Jewish woman in a time when that was a sentence of death. She did not choose to die with her people or for her people. She died because the Nazis came to the door of the convent and the Carmelites, though they tried, were unable to save her and her sister from the transport headed east.

Patricia Riley wrote a letter to *The New York Times* reasoning that Edith Stein had died a Catholic because her death was the direct result of the bishops of Holland having issued a statement two weeks before she was rounded up complaining about Nazi treatment of Jewish citizens of Holland. The act against Edith Stein is seen as a reprisal against Catholics for the statement they made on the behalf of Jews.

It was clearly honorable of the bishops of Holland to make this statement and Edith Stein may or may not have been picked up because of Nazi anger with the clergy, but that still does not change the primary cause of her difficulty. The only reason she was singled out of all the other Carmelite nuns who might also have been ready for martyrdom, beatification, and candidacy for sainthood was because she was a Jew.

It sticks in the Jewish throat, this proposed sainthood, because it slights other Jews, many of whom also wrote philosophical tracts, literary criticism, works of religious scholarship, art history, and medical research, poetry, cookbooks, and love letters. It sticks in the craw because of all the Jewish children who didn't have a chance to grow up and offer their own intellects to the world. It disturbs not because Edith Stein chose another religion but because she could not escape her birth certificate. Her religious commitment was a private matter and from all accounts the sincere choice of an outstanding philosophical intellect, but she did not die by choice, with honor, with dignity, with purpose, religious or otherwise. She simply died like the others. If the Church chooses her for special recognition, it is saying indirectly that the death of a Catholic means something special, deserves special recognition. Whatever the simple and respectful Catholic wish to honor a victim of oppression, the appearance is given that the Church believes her soul and her body had some value above the others.

The pope clearly hopes to spread the word of her martyrdom and in so doing to make clear the horror of the Holocaust while underlining the injustice of all anti-Semitism. However, for the Jewish community this beatification separates the deaths. It makes of Edith Stein's final moments a greater tragedy than the death of her unknown classmates in grammar school. And to the Jewish mind, in the democracy of the camps, there were no favored ones, except those who managed to live.

The recognition of Edith Stein, now on the second rung of the ladder to sainthood, serves also to blur the singularity of the Jewish tragedy. If Edith Stein is a saint, then the Holocaust becomes a general disaster belonging to Catholics as well as Jews. The Nazis never intended to rid the world of every last Catholic. They did not believe that Catholic women and children were a cancer in the public body. The Catholic Church in whose sanctuary Nazi war criminals slept should not yet make a Catholic saint out of a Jewish intellectual whatever her religious convictions.

The pope in October 1982 had elevated to sainthood Father Maksymilian Kolbe who had also died in Auschwitz. He had given his life for that of a Polish inmate who was a husband and father and was released when Father Kolbe was killed. This altruistic act certainly deserves notice in a selfish world, but Father Kolbe was a nationalist of great fervor. His objection to the Nazis was nationalistic not moral, and prior to the invasion he was the editor of a famous anti-Semitic newspaper that had a wide circulation. A known anti-Semite, even one caught in the machinery to kill the Jews, hardly seems a candidate for sainthood, at least to Jews. In making a pilgrimage to the camp and marking the death of Father Kolbe, the pope seems once again to diminish the death of all the unmentioned Jews who died there. When the pope also takes a Jewish woman who died as a Jewish woman and claims her death for the Church, one fears that the future will become confused as to what really happened and to whom.

The Carmelite nunnery is another problem between Catholics and Jews. Plans for it have now been changed and the Church is considering moving the nunnery to a site several miles away from the camp. The worship of the nuns will likely be as valid. Considering the vast spaces of the universe, those few miles cannot make much difference in the traveling of prayers.

In a meeting with Congressman Stephen Solarz on Jewish concerns about the convent, one Father Musial said that the Jewish community should see the convent as "a sign of our sickness and the sickness of Christians during the war. The convent should be a reminder to us of our present sickness and the need to do much better in the future. In building the convent we are not expiating the sins of others but our own sins." This may be so, but it hardly removes Jewish anxiety. Mr. Yitzak Arad, chairman of Yad Vashem, said after conducting Cardinal O'Connor through the memorial museum in Jerusalem, "All of us know about the silence of the Church at that time. If the Church had raised its voice many more Jews would have survived. It would have caused more Christians to help Jews and Jewish survival often depended on the local population." This piece of information complicates the matter and explains Jewish discomfort with Catholic prayers at the crematoria.

Father Musial, trying to convince the assembled rabbis and leaders of Jewish organizations of the benign nature of the convent, went on to say, "The convent gives new meaning to the camp itself. It is like a light, although sunlight is exterior to a room it shines in and enables people to see things in the room quite well." Ah, yes, but it is not as if Jews and Catholics and others cannot see what happened at Auschwitz with clarity. It is not as if the camp must have new meaning. It means what it means. New meaning is just what the Jewish community is wary of. In a meeting called to discuss the proposed Carmelite plan, a rabbi said, "This is a symbolic issue to me. Auschwitz is not a sacred place." And the symbol here is a rather ambiguous one. If the nuns pray for the Catholics who died at Nazi hands, and there were many, and for the Jews, and the Gypsies and the Poles and the homosexuals and all of God's creatures who didn't make it to 1945, then they are subsuming the Jewish tragedy into the whole and denying the particular intention of the concentration camp, designed to rid the world of Jews: that others could be conveniently disposed of once the machinery was in place is unquestionable. But the intention, the plan, the war, was against the Jewish population and the Carmelite nunnery perched at the site, near the great stones that mark the villages that are no more, what would it be but an uninvited mourner, a mourner who did not call out as the murderer proceeded in full daylight down the block with his murder weapon in hand, a mourner who had in other times spread slander about the victim, encouraged his isolation, taught the little children in her care that the victim had committed a terrible crime against a loved one in the family. True, some in the would-be-mourner's family had been killed by the murderer. Before anyone can accuse the would-be mourner of guilt through silence, she loudly points out her own family members who lie dead. Such a mourner really should not be permanently at the grave, however much sunlight she intends to bring.

There have been other misunderstandings. Cardinal O'Connor said to Zevulun Hammer, minister of religious affairs of Israel, "It might well be that the Holocaust may be an enormous gift that Judaism has given to the world. The suffering taught the world the sacredness and dignity of every human person." These words were instantly blinking on the wire services, and the Jewish leadership in New York reacted with haste and anger by sending Cardinal O'Connor, who had been walking a diplomatic tightrope since his trip to Israel began, a letter complaining about his use of the word gift. The Jews of course had no intention of offering such a gift: a present of six million men, women, and children, and the language offended. But the cardinal was offended that the Jews were offended because in his theology, to suffer, to offer to God a gift of suffering, was to imitate Christ, to become holy.

Rabbi Arthur Herzberg, Professor of Religion at Dartmouth College, says, "The Catholics have great difficulty admitting the Jewish nature of the Holocaust because of the basic tenets of their theology. At the center of the unknowable mystery, the mystical heart of Catholicism, is the belief that God sacrificed one third of Himself for the redemption of humankind. Jesus Christ is one third of the Holy Trinity. The concept of suffering as both a quality of God's and a sign of redemption is at the core of Catholic belief. When the Jews lost one third of their living body to the cross of Auschwitz it reawakened the question that maybe they really are God's chosen people. It is a replay of the Holy Mystery, but this time it bypasses the followers of Jesus Christ and concerns the people who have always claimed a special covenant with God. It is far more comfortable to declare the tragedy a European one, a universal one, than to confront the fact that it was the Jews who this time performed the Holy function of sacrifice."

While the constant Jewish condition, suffering has never been formally incorporated into Jewish theology. Jews know too much about pain to sanctify it.

It is understandable that the visiting cardinal, who had practically stood on his head to avoid insulting his Jewish hosts, and in addition was being reined in by a Vatican that does not have diplomatic relations with Israel and didn't want its cardinal looking like an official representative of the Church meeting formally with heads of state, could very reasonably have been exasperated by the demands of these Jews for whom nothing ever seems enough. He had said, after all, after leaving Yad Vashem, "Anything I would say here is banal. This experience is totally indescribable, I can't talk about it. It is a mystery to me." He was clearly moved and simply could not be accused of indifference or insensitivity.

He had invoked the Holocaust in his antiabortion cause. His position on abortion may be questioned, his right to use the Holocaust for this purpose may be challenged, but the sincerity and grief he feels seem indisputable. He said, "The Holocaust has chilled me ever since the first day I put my hand into the ovens at Dachau. The Holocaust has deepened my commitment to the sacredness of every human person. That is why I speak out so passionately about the unborn because I think they're human. This is why I speak about the crippled, and diseased, about Jews and Asians." The first part of this statement speaks about the cardinal's true empathetic concern about the Holocaust. The second, while stemming naturally from the first from the cardinal's point of view, is disturbing to Jews. There is something disconcerting here about the coupling in the same phrase the crippled and diseased and the Jews and Asians. The Nazis, of course, made the same association, and it is a bit worrisome even if well meant. While we know that the cardinal truly feels that the aborted fetus is human life, it is somewhat unseemly of him to use the Holocaust to make this point. Because the majority view in Jewish tradition does not consider nonviable life in the womb to be sacrosanct, and the use of the death of so many Jews to fuel, to evoke the horror and provoke the sympathy for the religious and political battle of pro-choice–pro-life, is a reduction of the meaning of the death in the camps, another kind of violation of the dead although intended in a cause the cardinal believes is good. Here is the cardinal speaking with great caring and feeling about the Holocaust and speaking within his religious framework and upsetting the Jews. It is almost impossible for a Catholic, no matter how well-intentioned, to speak of the Holocaust without scraping across raw nerves.

In 1987 the pope went to a synagogue in Rome and spoke to the congregation there of the horrors of the Holocaust and of the necessity of preventing it from ever happening again. Reconciliation seemed possible: here was the Catholic Church inside a Jewish synagogue, the Church allied with the people of the Word, Jewish tradition, Jewish life. Pope John Paul's physical presence was a mark of protection over the whole Jewish community. If the pope who had been pope when the Nazis came to Rome had also gone to that same synagogue and insisted that he must be rounded up with the other citizens of the Italian state, what then? But this present pope arrived only forty-five years late. It is as if the actions of the world leaders, saying the right things at the right gravesite, standing at memorials, lighting candles, are like the soap boats we used to send out to sea as children. They supply the romantic imagination with images but they cannot be boarded for a journey with a real destination.

And there is Kurt Waldheim, a Catholic and president of Austria, with whom the pope has met without referring to his Nazi past. He has been barred from American shores because of a hidden past as a Nazi officer in Yugoslavia at the time that partisans and Jews were sent off to their deaths, a past he had conveniently covered when working at the United Nations and becoming, so clever this man, the secretary general of the organization entrusted to bring peace to the nations of the world. The record of his past sat in closed files in a sealed room in the United Nations library.

He managed to bury this blot on his record until now. Of course, he was young. He was following orders not initiating them, but how well he must have done his job: what was his job exactly? Those were other times, other philosophies were fighting for world dominance. He did his thesis on a political scientist who had anticipated some of Hitler's favorite ideas. But that does not mean he anticipated the Final Solution in full flower. It does not mean that having seen the result of Nazi thinking he cannot change his views. He argues that he now supports human rights and the dignity of all peoples to live together in peace. Jews may be inclined to believe him, but not to honor him.

Now when the pope meets with Waldheim the Jewish community reacts with anger. They are reminded that Jewish life is not high on the list of political agendas. The pope who has expressed sympathy for the poor of Latin America, for the unborn the world around, for the hungry in Africa, for the oppressed in Poland, that same pope met with Waldheim and made no public statement about his past.

The American Jews responded with outrage. They wrote letters, protested outside the Vatican, made their complaint very clear. They went to talk things over with the pope at his summer palace. They threatened not to meet with him in Miami, but they did, and the pope, while still not recognizing Israel, said all the right things about the Holocaust and promised to start a dialogue with the Jewish community to work out the problems, the problems of Christian liturgy, of Christian doctrine that divide them. These meetings are surely Holocaust responses. Imagine the pope in 1939 meeting with a band of disgruntled Jews who didn't like his shaking the hand of Hitler's emissary to the Vatican.

Why, one wonders, is this pope suddenly concerned about not offending the Jews? Why did he seem conciliatory in Miami. Could this be conscience? Maybe. But some Jewish leaders believe that the same atheism, secularism of the world that pulled the Vatican toward the Nazis now pulls them toward the Jews. The Catholic hierarchy is feeling isolated, left out of the modern world, perhaps not as significant as they once were and surely their place, their power, has shrunk. The Jews appear to them, as they peep out from behind their confessionals, as allies, spiritual people in a non-spiritual time, allies in a Judeo-Christian tradition against the Moslem fundamentalists. One Jewish leader who has met with Vatican representatives says that Catholics now see the Jews as part of their tradition, as engaged in problems of the same God and His revelation. The Jews at a moment in Western history when all religion appears shaky take on qualities they may have lacked before.

Even so it is hard for the Catholics not to continually insult the Jews, through the beatification of Edith Stein, through the mollifying of Waldheim and the Austrian Catholics, through the statements, well meant or not, of various cardinals implying Jewish theological error or a Jewish destiny to suffer for others. The New York cardinal carries bedpans for AIDS patients. The Catholics have a tradition of washing the feet of the lepers and tending the misery of the world, miseries sometimes so ugly only a Catholic can face them, like Mother Teresa among the dying beggars of India. But the feelings of all the Jews in the world still weigh on some Vatican scale like a single feather of a bird shot in yesterday's hunt. That seems to be the reality. Even while Catholics are trying to build a bridge between the two groups, they go knocking at the supports, weakening the rivets.

At a dinner party, an Austrian Catholic woman expresses her anger at *The New York Times* for reporting on Waldheim. "They have discriminated against him. They have blown this matter all out of proportion," she says. "They are doing something just like anti-Semitism when they attack Waldheim that way. What they have done is worse than anti-Semitism." Some of the guests at the table nod their heads. The woman hates the socialists in Vienna and admires Waldheim because of his economic views. The Jewish issue annoys her. It is irrelevant to her concerns. For her the Holocaust is an irritant. The Jews and the protectors of the Jews are guilty of the crimes they accuse others of, she claims. The Jewish media have attacked Waldheim in a way even more vicious than Hitler's anti-Semitism. She wants no guilt. The Jewish guests at the table want her to feel guilty, to be ashamed of what happened. She wants the Jewish guests to be guilty of a crime so that the slate of conscience can be wiped clean. She wants no more of this Jewish matter. She is probably a good Catholic. The Catholic Church in Austria welcomed the Anschluss. She knows this but doesn't want to take the blame. She wants Waldheim honored so that she can feel honored, or at least no longer dishonored. She does not like Jews having the moral high ground. It places her on the low ground. At this dinner party we have the illusion of breaking bread together. In fact we eat alone.

The Vatican has not yet recognized Israel. First there was some question of a state with vague borders. But the Vatican recognizes other countries whose borders are in dispute. Then there was the question of the danger to Catholic citizens living in Arab lands, but the Vatican has diplomatic means to protect Catholic communities in Arab lands. Arabs after all do not attack Frenchmen, Germans, Japanese who live in or visit their countries just because these countries have recognized Israel. Christians in Lebanon have been attacked for reasons that have more to do with Lebanese tribal warfares than with Israel. The problem for the Vatican in recognizing Israel has been primarily a theological one. Catholic position has been that the Jews were driven from the land of Israel because they did not accept Jesus as their Savior and they are not to return until they do. If exile is punishment, then the Vatican weakens its dogma by recognizing the State of Israel, a Jewish state. Here is a meeting point of theology and politics.

The Jewish need for a Jewish state, born at the Dreyfus

trial, nourished in the early years of the twentieth century, brought to an imperative by the Holocaust, runs directly counter to the Catholic religious position, while not running counter to the Catholic expressed interest in dialogue and friendship with the Jews. In Miami in the fall of 1987, the pope did say that there was no theological reason not to recognize Israel. But he still has not done it. It seems probable that while officially removing the theological roadblock he was not able to remove the psychological debris that so many centuries of conviction had created. For the pope, political issues, attitudes in the Third World countries where the Church has a presence, again weigh more heavily than the wishes of the Jews. The pope met with Arafat, considered by most Jews to be a mere terrorist, their archenemy, the symbol of destruction. True the Palestinians are a suffering people with real wounds that need addressing, but without the prior recognition of the State of Israel, a meeting with Arafat seems like betrayal and it might seem so even to a people who had not been so often betrayed.

And the Jew: there are meetings with high-level Catholic officials, and our organization presidents in our cities all have interfaith breakfasts together, and all ask each other to speak to their respective congregations, but nevertheless, at bottom, the Jew still believes that the majority of Catholic leadership would abandon the Jews if the next Gestapo came, faster than the act of contrition is forgotten by the contrite. In the back of his mind as the music of interfaith harmony swells, the Catholic is thinking about souls and wondering if the Jew will be saved, will appear in the eternal world. The Jew is thinking about ways to ensure his physical, this worldly, social and communal safety. Jews do not accept the basic tenets of Christian belief, and the Catholics must believe, if they accept their own words, that the

Jews are locked out of the hereafter, and this so easily slides over into locking them out in the present. No wonder there are still frequent misunderstandings.

From the Catholic view these Jews must be a severe annoyance. They persist in bringing up the Holocaust. They scream when you try to present the disaster in its broadest sense, as a catastrophe for decent Europeans, as the murder of Poles, and Czechs and the crippled and diseased and Gypsies. They think only of themselves. They want the full glory of the martyrdom for themselves. They accuse the Church of crimes of omission when the Church annals are full of stories of priests who sacrificed and Catholics who risked all to save a few Jews. They presume to tell the most holy pope, who has a more direct line to God than most, just what he should do, whom he should meet with and to whom he should grant the posthumous Catholic prizes. They are as stubborn now as they were in the early centuries of this millennium. Members of their religion have been prominent enemies of social order and religious truth since the early days of the nineteenth century. They produced that renegade Jew, Freud, who thought God was no more than man's wish to be cradled in his mother's arms, who argued that religion was created by man and not by God. They produced Marx, who said the Church was the master of ceremonies for the circus of the rich. Marx was the renegade Jew who spread atheism and damnation across the globe. Do we believe that those two false prophets' avowed lack of conventional religion made them less Jewish? Not for a moment. These Jews, believing or not, produce revolution and subversion in a thousand paintings and a thousand books. We are never free of them and our only consolation is that they are never free of us. Jews are a race of people who stand outside and point at us and yet seem attached to us like our feet or our hands; they will not slip quietly into the past. Think what a different turn history would have had if the Jews were like the Hittites and had accepted defeat and sent those perverse genes into oblivion. On all accounts that would have been better: so many would have been spared suffering.

The official organizations, Jewish and Catholic, work for understanding, for interfaith cooperation, for increased mutual respect, and all that is good work, necessary work, if a little thankless. Rabbi Abraham Joshua Heschel went to meet with Catholic hierarchy in the last years of his life. He said that he regretted not having made more attempts at contacting them in Berlin before the war, that lives might have been saved had dialogues between religious leaders begun in time. Possibly. Of course Jews must believe and act on Heschel's concern to open communications, but people, Jews and Catholics, with rare exceptions, continue to nurture their suspicions of each other, water them with jokes and tales of the past, and will live peacefully side by side only as long as the values of a pluralistic society hold. But relying on the structures of pluralism, recent history has shown us, is like depending on sandbags to keep the rushing river from overflowing its banks—sometimes it works, sometimes it fails—and when it fails, the Catholics and the Protestants bomb each other as in Northern Ireland or the Tamils and the Sikhs gun down their Hindu or Moslem neighbors who in turn repeat the bloodshed, and in this century the rivers have been rising and flooding everywhere. We have to worry about the effectiveness of the most well-intentioned acts of friendship across the tribal divide. It is as easy to make people tolerant as it is to make them chaste.

But sometimes it happens. Michael Fabricus, a German history student at the Johann Gutenberg University in

Mainz, speaking in New York in the winter of 1988, said that the facts of the Holocaust enforced his Catholicism, because it showed the need for religious and moral belief. He says "the knowledge of the Holocaust has inspired my interest in ecumenical things, my hopes for a tolerant religion." He believes that in the future the Catholic Church should be active in fighting against prejudice. He says that "the failure of the Catholic Church to be active in promoting the fight against the Holocaust motivates me not to be stubborn about religions but to search out the things that all religions share in common." His support of Turkish workers and other foreigners in Germany today is determined, he believes, by what he knows about the Holocaust. These feelings expressed by a young German, they too are a part, a more hopeful part of the Catholic-Jewish dialogue that goes on today.

Jewish organizations will go on doing what they do to pressure the pope to recognize Israel, to recognize the thin skin of Jewish sensibility. Catholics, now existing in a world in which they are neither the rulers nor the only and final moral authority, will surely continue to listen. It is essential that Catholics understand the Jewish need not to have the Holocaust preempted and turned into a general human tragedy. Perhaps in several generations it will be possible to think of the victims of the Holocaust as Jews and non-Jews in one human category, but for the Jews of today it is important the graves not be desecrated by a premature call to universalism. The Catholics will have to live with the fact that the Jews were martyred. Jews stand like David fighting against Goliath, an unsuccessful David, to be sure, but a David who died on the moral high ground. Catholics will have to come to terms with the fact that the Catholic peoples of Germany and Austria and elsewhere welcomed Hitler into power and they share some indirect cultural guilt at the calamity that followed. The more one tries to ignore the Jewish issues that have come forward in this post-Holocaust era, the more they stir and boil, requiring answers.

Jews will have to see that this matter of guilt makes Catholics uneasy and angry. In truth, collective guilt is always unfair, and this Holocaust guilt that lies behind the Church's desire to universalize the dead is also unfair to the living.

If Catholics are more forthcoming in discussing what happened in 1939–1945, if they make a clear statement about the official silence, if they recognize the State of Israel, then perhaps the Jews will stop causing guilt, stop going over the past. Jews sometimes now react too fast and with their own lack of understanding of Catholic positions. The divisions have lasted for nearly two thousand years and the healing will only come slowly and in small steps. The difference in actual religious vision may prevent the participants in this dialogue from ever fully accepting one another. The only hope is for each side to imagine itself as the other, feel what pinches, what shames, what hurts. In any event it will take many years for the mutual angers to cool and for the issues of the Holocaust to recede far enough so that they may stop burning the tongues that speak.

Russians and Jews

NEXT YEAR IN JERUSALEM

It is hard to understand why the Soviets are still at it, still making life hard for the Jews who live within their borders. The history of the Jews in Russia is violent and sad enough without this contemporary chapter.

In 1550, Czar Ivan IV declared, "It is not convenient to allow Jews to come with their goods into Russia, since many evils result from them, for they import poisonous herbs and lead astray Russians from Christianity." In 1563, immediately after the Russian conquest of Polotsk, Czar Ivan ordered that all Jews who refused baptism should be drowned. In 1610 all Jews were forbidden to enter Moscow on business. In 1648 the Cossack leader Bogdan Chmielnicki led a Cossack revolt against the Polish gentry. His followers turned against the Jews and killed 100,000 of them; many more were tortured and raped. In 1744 the Empress Elizabeth expelled the Jews from Livonia—35,000 Jews were driven out in nine years. In 1795 the laws were passed that confined the Jews to the Pale. The poverty that arose in those small towns was fierce. Almost a quarter of the Jews living there were on relief. Throughout the nineteenth century there were sporadic pogroms against the communities in the Pale: typical are the documents from Balta which record that in March of 1882, forty were killed and twenty rapes occurred. In 1837 the burning and banning of Jewish books in St. Petersburg set off a further set of attacks on

Jewish communities. In 1823 Czar Alexander issued an edict forbidding the Jews of Russia to own land in any village towns or keep hotels or inns. This law led to the expulsion of 20,000 Jews into towns where many became vagrant beggars. In 1882, 500,000 Jews living in rural areas of the Pale were forced to leave their homes and live in towns and shtetls in the Pale; 250,000 Jews living along the western frontier of Russia were moved into the Pale; 700,000 Jews in all were driven into the Pale by 1891. That same year 2,000 Jews were driven from St. Petersburg, many in chains; 20,000 Jews were expelled from Moscow. These are the figures. Imagine them in human terms.

Despite these edicts, which were sporadically enforced, Jews did manage to settle in Russia. A vibrant and thriving Jewish intellectual and spiritual life grew despite poverty and continued oppression by the authorities, including a demand that Jewish boys serve in the army of the czar for twenty-five years. Hasidic life, rabbinic tradition, thrived, despite or perhaps because of the vital disagreements between different Jewish branches, those more turned toward the Enlightenment and those more spiritual and mystical.

The trial of Mendl Bellis in 1913, in which a Jew was accused of ritual murder of a Christian child, offered a spectacle equal to the Dreyfus carnival and one that should have served as an alarm, a sounding of the depth of the people's dislike of Jews and the perilous nature of Jewish breath in and out of the Pale. It was clear enough at the time that the Black Hundreds, the Russian Right, was ready to do anything, commit any perjury, stage any witch trial to spread the murderous urge against Jews. Leon Pinsker, a Jewish physician writing in 1882, says, "We do not count ourselves as a Nation among the other nations and we have no voice in the council of peoples even in affairs that concern ourselves. Our Fatherland is an alien country, our unity: dispersion, our solidarity: the general hostility to us, our weapon: humility, our defense: flight and our originality: adaptability, our future: tomorrow. What a contemptible role for a people that once had its Maccabees." Jewish defense groups did form but they were not able to protect the communities. And the Maccabees were sorely missed and the Messiah was eagerly awaited in the Russian towns in which Jews lived.

In the early years of this century, the Ukrainians, along with the Cossacks, turned against their Jewish neighbors. At Kishinev in 1903, 49 Jews were murdered, 15,000 Jewish shops and homes were demolished. In Odessa, in the month of October 1905, 300 Jews were killed and thousands were driven out of their homes. There were 790 separate pogroms between 1900 and 1905, and these drove hundreds of thousands into flight. Yiddish songs spoke of the tragedy: "Shout Jews, Shout as Loud as you can, So loud your shout reaches on high, His sleep is just a lie. What's He trying to put over? What are we, flies in the wind? Is there nothing in our favor? Enough, it's got to end." And this was forty years before it really began! The poet Bialik, sent to Kishinev to collect eyewitness accounts of the tragedy, wrote a poem called "In the City of Slaughter." Yiddish poetry, novels, began to tell of unbearable human suffering, of endless murders in a desolate landscape.

In World War I whole communities were swept away, uprooted as potential enemy spies, attacked by armies of all nations, and thousands upon thousands died of hunger, as well as the typhoid that spread quickly through crowded ghettos. Some Jews were murdered by anarchists, some by Bolsheviks, some by White Russians. Wherever there was murder, there was rape, and children were orphaned and starved and capriciously killed.

Just before the revolution the Russian intellectuals were becoming sympathetic to the Jewish community and calling for an end to the discriminatory laws that deprived them of rights available to other citizens. After the revolution the limitations on Jews were lifted. Jewish life had a brief moment of resurgence and Zionist groups formed, as well as publishing houses, defense groups, and literary societies, and Jews were permitted into secular education everywhere. The moment was brief. In 1918 the Jewish societies were closed for not conforming to the Spirit of the Times. The new policy was to forcibly assimilate Jews as well as other national groups into the Soviet state. In 1919 under the leadership of Simon Petlyura, over 60,000 Jews were murdered by Ukrainian nationalists and anti-Bolsheviks. This was the worst massacre in Russia since the pogroms of 1648: so moral progress in Russia, as elsewhere, was running on a reverse track.

In 1927 the Hasidic leader Rabbi Joseph Schneerson was imprisoned and expelled from Russia. In 1928 all Hebrew books were banned from publication and Zionist and Jewish writers were imprisoned or exiled to Central Asia. In 1934 the Jewish poet Osip Mandelshtam was arrested for writing a satiric poem about Stalin. His arrest caused renewed anti-Semitism in the country. He died in the Gulag. At the time of the Stalin-Hitler pact there were mass arrests of Zionists, Bundists, religious Jews, and Jewish writers. In the Stalin purges of 1937 many thousands of Jews were executed, way out of proportion to their numbers in the population at large.

During World War II, 500,000 Jews served in the Soviet army; 200,000 of them were killed in action. The Nazis shot or gassed in vans 500,000 Jews, men, women, and children. While it is true that Jews were safer in Russia than in any other Western country during the period of the Nazi invasions and official policy condemned anti-Semitism, Jews nevertheless suffered from the attitudes of anti-Semitism that were endemic in local populations. At a time when extremes of brutality could hardly be noticed in the general carnage, the Ukrainian townspeople, only twenty-two years after their own massacre of Jews, did little to help their neighbors who were rounded up by the Nazis, marched into nearby forests, and buried in long trenches that heaved hours after the last of the Einsatzgruppen, as reported in Martin Gilbert's book *The Holocaust,* had gone back to their lodgings to write long letters home to their wives and mothers and girlfriends. Jews who fled to the forests and joined the resistance were sometimes welcomed by partisan groups and sometimes they were shot. And after the war, there were purges of Jewish party members, attacks on Jews prominent in literature and medicine that resulted in the death of many and the banishment of others. In Vilna in 1944 after the liberation of the city by Soviet troops, the authorities forbade the setting up of any Jewish organizations and arrested many Jews who wished to emigrate to Palestine. In Kiev on the nineteenth of November 1944, following the city's liberation by the Soviet army, an anti-Jewish pogrom broke out despite or perhaps because of the massacre of more than 100,000 Jews at Babi Yar only three weeks before. In 1947 in Kharkov, Rabbi Lev was arrested after refusing to become an informer on fellow Jews. Synagogues were closed all over Russia. In 1946, in Berdichev, the Soviet Yiddish writer Vasily Grossman was refused permission to publish his *Black Book* of Nazi crimes against Soviet Jewry.

How could this happen after the war when one would have thought the horror of the Holocaust would have forced

Russian anti-Semites to pause and consider? The Holocaust may have had less immediate impact in Russia because of the mass deaths that the Stalinists had inflicted on all people before the war and the carnage of the Eastern Front which must have itself seemed like an end to civilization: the death camps then being only a variant of the common and nationally experienced terror. But the Holocaust *has had* an effect on the Soviet position toward Jews, one that has become clearer in recent years.

In the Communist state after the war anti-Semitism still boiled in the body politic because there was so much to be angry about, so great a need to blame somebody, so great a need to avenge the disasters of the war, and the Jews as usual were there, albeit in smaller numbers than ever before, to absorb blame, to take communal punishment. The Russian bureaucrats were able to manipulate anti-Semitism to forge the Soviet people together, to distract from government failures, to provide a safety valve for the disappointments of a faulty system. In 1952 in Crimea fifty-two Jewish leaders and authors were executed on charges of wanting to secede Crimea from the Soviet Union. In 1953 many prominent doctors were arrested and accused of plotting to kill Soviet leaders. Since the majority of the arrested doctors were Jewish, this sparked a wave of anti-Semitism that spread throughout the country, causing Jews to be excluded from some universities and to lose jobs in the bureaucracy. In Leningrad Chief Rabbi Labanov was sentenced to five years in prison and Rabbi Epshtein to ten years for the crime of religious activity. Haydim Lensky, one of Stalin's victims who languished in Siberian exile for writing in Hebrew, said in one of his poems, "A new barber—a new order. What remains is the same old razor." When in the 1960s the Soviets began executing people for economic crimes, Jews, who were only 2 percent of the population, were 86 percent of those arrested and executed for such matters as speculation in shoes or fruit.

The folk anti-Semitism of the 1950s in Russia was also connected to the Russian fear of the Jews, a fear of vengeance. Some Russians feared Jews as if they were ghosts come back to haunt, to remind Russians of what happened to Jews on Russian soil. Martin Gilbert reports in his book *The Holocaust* that "Twenty years following the war, Babi Yar filled up with rubbish, mud and water forming a deep lake. Above the Yar a wall had been built to mark it off from an adjoining brick yard. One evening in 1961 the wall collapsed. Streams of clay and mud, mixed up with the remains of human bones, gushed out into the streets of Kiev below. Fires broke out and the stream of liquid clay buried alive tramworkers and passengers. Twenty-four citizens of Kiev were killed. A few days later as the tram passed the site of the disaster an old woman called out, 'It's the Jews who have done this, they are taking their vengeance, they always will.' A taxi driver told his passenger, 'One could not fill up the Babi Yar. Jewish Blood is taking revenge.' "

The poet Andrei Voznesensky, writing in the 1980s, described in a poem called "The Ditch" the massacre of 12,000 Soviet Jewish citizens in the Crimea by the Nazi elite troops and the contemporary plundering of the graves by the local Soviet citizens. The large gravesite lies just outside of Simferopol, the Crimean capital. It has near it a small monument commemorating the deaths but nowhere on that monument is the word Jew. The poem in translation reads in part, "A war will spread out of there, / Don't cut out the spiritual spores with your spades. / Something more terrible than the plague will come out of there." The local population had begun digging up bodies at night and taking out gold teeth, stripping wedding bands that had been hidden in now-decayed bits of clothing, finding tiny fragments of jewelry. These grave robbers were tolerated by the local authorities, Voznesensky believes, because the bodies were Jewish bodies, and these were a dead that needed no respect, that needed to be killed for sure a second time.

All the Russian cities and villages in which Jews had lived have holes in them, spaces where Jewish life had been, and the Jews who remain, the Jews who came back, the Jews who survived, are older, fewer, and less Jewish. What is to be feared from them now? Why not just let the Jews go, those who want to emigrate, those who want to learn Hebrew? Let it be over, the history of persecution of Jews on Russian soil.

Experts in the field of Soviet Jewish relations believe that the KGB doesn't want to let any group out. They believe that this would signal a weakness of the state, loss of control. But the Soviet government has not been entirely consistent on this matter. They did let some of the Germans out in a deal with the West German government. They have let some Jews go, in response to world pressure, to continued Jewish protest from within, sporadically, whimsically, using excuses such as possession of state secrets to keep others. The Soviets do not recognize the State of Israel and so no special arrangement can be made. Emigration of large numbers of Westernized Jews to Israel would be considered a hostile act by Arab countries, and so the balances of world politics work to seal the borders. At least that is the political excuse. The real reasons may lie deeper. For the Soviets, any emigration is an act of treason. Any large-scale emigration, and it is possible that anywhere between 100,000 and 500,000 Jews would emigrate if the doors were opened, would be an admission to the world that the Soviet state is less than paradise. Furthermore, there is a real demographic anxiety that the Russians, whose birthrate is low, will soon be overwhelmed by their Moslem citizens, and the wish to hold on to the Jewish population is a wish to hold on to those who are not Moslems, as well as to prevent what Soviet General Secretary Mikhail Gorbachev has suggested would be a brain drain since so many Jews have performed outstandingly in science and technology. The Soviet fear of the nationalisms within the state focuses on the Jews, who have always been accused of cosmopolitanism because they indeed have loyalties that cross the best-guarded borders. In trying to clarify the Soviet motives one always comes to a point where rationality stumbles and we have to assume that the Soviet attitude toward Jewish emigration is based on its own mythology and demonology and has its roots in the history of the two peoples more than in any pragmatic matter.

The release of Jews has become a bargaining chip for the commissars in charge who hope to obtain concessions from the West in matters of trade or in the political-military arena, and so they alter the number of those permitted exit with the varying breezes of détente. In the years 1970 to 1976, 118,000 Jews were granted exit visas. In the years 1977 to 1980, another 119,000 flew to Vienna and on to Israel or America. But then as détente soured with the Soviet invasion of Afghanistan and President Ronald Reagan's attacks on the Evil Empire, the numbers dwindled and emigration was virtually choked off. As in ancient Judaea the fate of the Jews waits on the doings of the great powers, and as in the ancient world this small group of people manages to rivet attention on their predicament, to take a role in the fortunes of empires, a role way out of proportion to their numbers or their intentions.

The Russian conflict with Jewish emigration, this opposition between state and ethnic loyalty that has gone right over the edge of official tempers, lies deep in the history of Russian-Jewish relations, and like a certain kind of bad marriage, a certain kind of sad intertwining of stories makes it particularly hard for the Russians just to turn away and let go.

The Russians have not allowed the word Jew to appear on war monuments. At Babi Yar there is a small plaque dedicated to the victims of Fascism, without any mention of the fact that some 98 percent of the 100,000 dead were killed because they were Jewish and only because they were Jewish. In 1965 when Rabbi Wolfe Kelman offered a prayer for the dead at Babi Yar, a group of Soviet citizens, possibly KGB, heckled him, denying that the dead were Jews. The fact that Russians have not admitted that something singular happened to their Jewish citizens during the war makes it hard for them now to admit the special and unique status of Jews in relation to the rest of the Soviet population. Since anti-Semitism as such is not given official approval, it must, claims the authorities, have disappeared, but the traditional prejudices of a people do not just disappear. Jewish refuseniks who have met with representatives of the American Jewish community have complained of anti-Semitic attitudes that affect their children's education and their advancement in careers. The 350,000 to 400,000 Jews who have received letters of invitation to live abroad from fellow Jews are hoping to live not only Jewish lives but ones free of the possible effects of prejudice.

Now that *glasnost* has made it possible for the people to begin to express some political feelings, a Rightist anti-Semitic organization called Pamyat is permitted to demonstrate thousands strong in the streets and to meet freely. On the other hand demonstrations of Jewish refuseniks are still curtailed by the authorities. The Pamyat organization is neo-Fascist and blames all of the Soviet economic and political problems on the Jews. This group is a reprise of the Black Hundreds that fueled anti-Semitism in the society in the late nineteenth and early twentieth centuries. The fact that during the war Jews were killed in such numbers in such a way makes them only more likely victims, only marks them out, as different, defenseless, unwanted. The Russian citizen may feel some residual and particular horror at the fate of the Jews, as well as some trace of guilt that stems from the long history of anti-Semitism in official and nonofficial Russia. The Jew as a tragic and martyred figure may be a reproach to the Russian who thinks of himself as the righteous victim of the Second World War. The Jew, by still existing, accuses the others, stands as a symbolic marker of what man can do to man. As a victim of state violence the Jew reminds the populace of the specifics, the details, the end result of the unchecked power of those whose power is granted by fiat. Whatever mysterious religious and economic clouds hung over Jewish heads before the Holocaust, today each Jew is an automatic reminder of maniacal violence.

Above all, the Russians do not want to deal with history. They attempted to confiscate the documents on the pogroms that were collected by Jews and smuggled out to Germany between the wars. Yuri N. Afanasyev, now under Gorbachev, the rector of the State Historical Archives Institute, says that "since Czarist days historians have been counted as part of the official establishment, their word regarded as a form of official prayer." Ilya Ehrenburg, who stayed alive while other Jewish intellectuals were executed, helped Vasily Grossman collect his *Black Book* of Nazi crimes against Jews in Russia. He continued to keep documents of Jewish suffering during the war and these have been brought to Israel, but they could not be published in the Soviet Union which has made a policy of not marking the particular Jewish fate under the Nazis.

This denial of the particular Jewish tragedy in World War II serves to deny the separate history of the Jews on Soviet soil and it covers up some bitter divisions among groups of Russians, some of whom supported the Nazis. Some Ukrainians served in the camps as kapos and as guards. They may have been anti-Communist and seeking liberation for themselves through an alliance with the Nazis, but nevertheless they are now part of the Soviet society and they once aided the Nazis. From the government point of view determined to unite the various ethnic groups under one Soviet banner, the less said about the past the better.

The unfortunate way the Russians have dealt with the deep and constant strain of violent anti-Semitism in their culture is by denying the importance and meaning of Jewish existence, of Jewish life, of Jewishness. The Jew cannot make them feel guilty, the Jew cannot make them deal with the real facts of history, if they don't acknowledge the reality of the Jew, if they make the subject altogether a non-subject. They do not acknowledge a special obligation to Jews because of past history because they do not admit the past history.

The suffering of all Russians under Hitler was mighty. Aside from the murders of civilians in the taking and the retaking of the cities, soldiers died in huge numbers and the citizenry suffered from hunger and cold and bombardments. The Nazis killed close to two million Russian prisoners of war. The Russians who lost so much in that war are not in any mood to pay special attention to Jewish suffering which was, as they see it, different in kind but in the end just human suffering the same as theirs.

The government has at times tried to force assimilation on all its ethnic subgroups. But the Jewish issue is especially fraught with meaning for Russian society. The people and the bureaucrats know, even as they deny that they know it, that the Jews carry a special history and are the target of special feelings of dislike.

Anti-Zionism is a real political fact in the Soviet global balancing act. It is also a veiled and new form of anti-Semitism. In 1953 the official Communist magazine *Krokodil* attacked in one article, American and British bankers, colonialists, armament kings, Nazi generals, and the Zionist conspiracy. On May 3, 1959, in a typical remark, *Pravda* referred to Israel as hell on earth. This anti-Zionism became the excuse for new arrests and for a further stirring of anti-Semitic feeling in the country at large. The Zionist loyalty of the refuseniks automatically placed them at odds with the Russian state.

The prominent refuseniks, those arrested, jailed, exiled, those who have banded together as part of the original Helsinki Human Rights Watch group, those who have become world famous because of efforts on the part of American and Israeli Jews to obtain their liberation, have come to represent in Russia and in the world the vision of human freedom. Ida Nudel, Vladimir Slepak, Begun, Lerner, Rubin, Berlin, the whole group of them who suffered persecution, who were brave enough to demonstrate in front of official buildings, who have resisted calling each other spies, who have withstood the best efforts of the regime to destroy their spirits and their movement, have become in their advocacy the first internal sign of resistance to dictatorship. They are sparking, in the best sense of a light unto the nations, the fight for individual rights.

Anatoly Shcharansky wrote in Christopol prison in 1979: "Hence my affirmation, borrowed from the existentalists and perceived by reason but not consciously, that freedom can neither be given nor taken away, since man is freedom, seems to me now as natural as life itself." Jews have become a major voice in confronting the Soviet state on its dishonesty, its treatment of its prisoners, on its laws that can be used to silence and repress. The Russian Jewish refusenik problem has managed to become a symbolic issue of human rights, a matter of freedom as opposed to oppression. It may be a bargaining chip on international tables but it is even more importantly a symbol of human cruelty, families separated, rights denied, imprisonment for ordinary religious wishes. The Jewish refusenik embodies the noblest of human hopes and through persistence mocks those cruel activities that continue around the globe in countries of the Left and of the Right who use brutality against dissent. That is why Jewish free emigration from the Soviet Union has taken on such weight in world affairs. Political arrangements sometimes are shaped by symbolic, even literary, dramatic matters. The Jews once again have become the unwilling heroes of an anti-authoritarian drama. After the Holocaust the Jews are a natural universal symbol for a people who suffer, who are subjected to tyranny, whose freedoms have been taken away. Their survival, from the days of slavery in Egypt, has carried a message of human hope woven through the sad tales of too many defeats.

Under *glasnost,* under world pressure, it is possible that the gates of exodus will be opened, or at least opened somewhat wider. It is also possible, given the capriciousness of the totalitarian mind, that those same gates may again slam shut. If the prominent troublemakers are granted release and the others are not, new spokespeople will arise inside Russia and the process will begin again. The more the Russians try to ignore the Jewish issue, the more it becomes a metaphor for the resistance to totalitarianism, and the more brave men and women become willing to risk everything for an exit visa, to teach Hebrew in their living rooms, to make matzoth at Passover. The Jewish issue now serves as a kind of hot coal that burns at the heart of the Soviet dictatorial regime.

The Jewish community as a whole serves a democratizing, liberalizing end. In the nineteenth century the great French intellectuals thought that Jewish life was backward, that it was hindering the forward march of reason and sat like a rock on the railroad tracks of progress ready to cause problems at each crossing. But they were wrong. Jewish life served rather to signal the need for humane and reasonable laws that would allow all groups their identity. Without an essential capacity to accept pluralism, many ideas, many ways of doing things, the torturers will continue to ply their trade in the cellars of prisons, in the halls of psychiatric hospitals, out of sight but not out of mind.

The lesson of the Holocaust is the value, the worth of every human life, the knowledge that when respect for individual human dignity disappears, savagery, bestiality, brutality, follow directly, debasing everything in the society. This is a lesson that Russia cannot yet hear. The Soviet Union cannot look too closely at the Holocaust because it will see its own ruthless face distorted there. No wonder they break the mirrors.

The Jew as object of anti-Semitism becomes the hated devil holding within his being all the known bad qualities of mankind, and yet the Jew of the Holocaust becomes the guilty conscience of the society. One could say this is the destiny of the Jews or less mystically this is the irony of the Jew, his continued existence reproaches those who hated him, who did terrible things to others, and their guilt and shame provoke anew the wish to eradicate, silence him one way or the other forever.

Until the Soviets are able to deal with their own history, the history of the Gulag, of the murders of writers and dissidents and farmers and neighbors and friends, they will not be able to approach the Holocaust as a historical reality. They will not be able to see their Jews as they are, some ready to rise and go to Israel, others willing to assimilate and join the Communist endeavor. They will have to keep denying the Jewish nature of the Holocaust, keeping the publication of materials, such as Grossman's *Black Book,* out of the hands of the public, allowing the play of Anne Frank only two days' production by an Italian troop, erasing Jewish identity from the base of monuments. It seems likely that until the Russians come fully to terms with their own lack of freedoms and their own bloody past, they will not be able to accept the Jewish application for freedom. It is easy to understand how difficult such a reckoning would be for the Russian state. Painful matters would be exposed, most having nothing to do with Jews. But as with most matters of confession and repentance, this is the way toward national sanity: the way toward healing. Perhaps it is beginning as certain Soviet leaders are reclaimed and others are reproved in this new revisionist wind that has come with Gorbachev. But then again perhaps this shift is no more than seasonal.

The Holocaust and Israel

THE PHOENIX RISES

The political situation in the Middle East is in such turmoil that new shapes, issues, forms, are now erupting almost daily. The Arabs in the occupied territories are expressing their despair and frustration with increased determination. The Jews are under attack to alter the status quo both from within and without. Whatever forms of political compromise will be achieved, whatever kind of arrangement, to whose benefit and whose grief, the fact is that the Holocaust has cast its long shadow over these conflicts. Solutions, ideal formulas for lasting peace, even modest proposals for an easing of the tensions, these will come from politicians, Israelis, Arabs, and those who exert some power, have some direct stake in the outcome. This book can only look backward at how the Holocaust has played its hand in matters unimagined by those who intended the Final Solution to be final.

After the war peoples all over the world were demanding autonomy and new states sprouted in the dry colonial soil. The Jews also got their state, but as always with Jews the matter was similar but not identical. The State of Israel owes the timing of its political reality directly to the Holocaust. Despite the Balfour Declaration, the shilly-shallying of the imperalist powers might have continued forever and the need for Arab oil, the joust between the East and West, might well have banished the Zionist dream into the heads of poets and prophets where it could spin on for another several millennia undisturbed. Here is Andrei Gromyko addressing the United Nations, on May 14, 1948, the day before independence: "—During the last war, the Jewish people underwent exceptional sorrow and suffering. Without any exaggeration, this sorrow and suffering are indescribable. It is difficult to express them in dry statistics on the Jewish victims of the fascist aggressors. The Jews in the territories where the Hitlerites held sway were subjected to almost complete physical annihilation.—The United Nations cannot and must not regard this situation with indifference, since that would be incompatible with the high principles proclaimed in its charter—The fact that no Western European State has been able to ensure the defense of the elementary rights of the Jewish people and to safeguard it against the violence of the fascist executioners explains the aspirations of the Jews to establish their own state. It would be unjust not to take this into consideration and to deny the right of the Jewish people to realize this aspiration."

Without the Holocaust, European Jews might well have continued to assimilate in large numbers, to intermarry and to grow roots so deep into the nation-states of a hundred countries they could never be transplanted. Without the Holocaust, American Jews might have lost even more of their members to the majority and the remnant would be waiting for the Messiah before flying to Jerusalem. The Zionist vision may have begun with Herzl but it became a reality with Hitler. The Holocaust changed the map of the Middle East. The Western countries in a moment of guilty conscience allowed Israel to exist, to end the Jewish problem, to pay homage to the dead who would not have died had there been an Israeli consulate to stamp visas and an Israeli prime minister who could pick up the phone and speak to the heads of state. And so inherent in the birth of Israel, intrinsic to the celebration of its nationhood, is the experience of the Holocaust. Nevertheless, the Zionist dream was not born with Hitler and the Jewish need for a state existed well before the twentieth century. The Holocaust forced the birth of the state by dramatically vindicating the Zionist vision, but that vision with its ancient religious root and its political urgency was not simply the product of the most recent tragedy but the extension of a long Jewish history.

Central to the Passover Haggadah is the Talmudic dictum that in each and every generation each person shall regard himself as though he personally had emerged from Egypt. This now symbolically stands for survival of the Holocaust, and the exodus from Europe to Israel. While many Israelis do not like to think of the Holocaust and many others have come from Arab states where its effect was less powerful and its threat less personal, still it remains behind the Israeli state, a presence, far greater than the Statue of Liberty in New York Harbor, perhaps even more binding than the U.S. Constitution. Israel is by no means the first nation in the world to have its birth attended by war, its borders in dispute, native populations under threat and expelled, but it is certainly the first nation to be born because the world agreed that a crime had been committed. Israelis might prefer other stories, wolves suckling twins and the like, but the fact is that modern Israel was touched and informed in all its beginnings by the inexplicable and implacable hatred of Jews in the Western nations of this world.

In Israel today ten public institutions are devoted to the Holocaust. On Yom Hoshoah, the Day of Remembrance, the state comes to a halt and mourns. In the Diaspora Museum the scroll of fire tells the story of Jewish persecution and resistance from the destruction of the Second Temple on, but its power lies in our knowledge of the Holocaust and the final destination of the communities whose names and whose synagogues we see. In Yad Vashem we see the Holocaust entire, we feel the Holocaust. Recently at the cost of eight million dollars a Valley of the Destroyed Communities has been set up to honor the children killed in the Holocaust. In the Diaspora Museum in Tel Aviv, we see replicas of synagogues, stories of towns and communities that were burned to the ground by Hitler's men.

If we can speak of the founding of America as a search for freedom, as a result of the Enlightenment, as a dream of a just society, or less romantically as a capitalistic venture, a poem to free enterprise, we can find in the birth of Israel the passionate cry of "never again," never again surrounded, ambushed, forgotten, burned, and destroyed. The Rightist Kach party led by Rabbi Meir Kahane, attempting to raise money from American Jews, said in an advertisement in *The New York Times,* "And let us not fear the world. Those who stood by during the Holocaust and when Israel faced destruction in 1948, in 1967, have nothing to tell us. Faith in the G-d of Israel and a powerful army are the only guarantors of Jewish survival. Let us not fear the world. Far better a Jewish state that survives and is hated by the world than an Auschwitz that brings us its love and sympathy." Kahane has only one seat in the Knesset. His party is not a major political force. But the point of view expressed in this statement is shared by many Israelis and by many American Jews. They are not interested in the emotional rewards of being good and nice and they do not want to be victims again. They are tired of pricking the conscience of the comfortable and safe majority of Christians and Moslems in this world. These are a people who have suffered and who are determined now to become masters instead of slaves, occupiers instead of the occupied. Israelis are accused of being particularly rude, rough, crude. The story is told about the Sabra who is hard outside, but inside, very hard. If "never again" is the womb of the state, then the nation needs and must have a warrior soul.

In 1987 Foreign Minister Shimon Peres, as reported in the *Jerusalem Post,* called on the Jews the world over to learn the lesson of the Holocaust. "Those who hesitate to come to Israel are likely to miss the opportunity." He was reminding all Jews of the necessity of Israel whose existence would save their lives if the maniacal forces of anti-Semitism rise again. He spoke to the natural fear that it will happen again and there will be nowhere to turn, no one to stamp an exit visa. He speaks to the words of critic George Steiner who wrote, "When I listen to my children breathing in the stillness of my house I grow afraid. I am utterly trying to teach my children the sense of vulnerability and keep them in training for survival." Shimon Peres, who wants aliyah (immigration) to strengthen Israel, knows how to use the Holocaust for his purposes, and while Jews in America and England and France may not pack up and move at his words, they hear them and they maintain their political activity on behalf of Israel. They follow the politics of the Middle East the way a cardiac patient attempts to read the moving lines on the machine by his bedside.

The Holocaust is used in Israel to support all sides of the political issue, to justify and descry, to rally and to calm, to criticize and to support the government. Professor Yishayahyu Libowitz of the Hebrew University thinks that the conquest of the West Bank may turn Israel into a Jewish Nazi state. Former Israeli prime minister Menachem Begin claimed that the alternative to fighting the PLO in Lebanon was Auschwitz again. The highly emotional words, Nazi, Auschwitz, Nuremberg, racist, Fascist, are bandied about the newspapers, in speeches, in policy directives. The Holocaust storms through Israeli life, picking up force from biblical events, from destructions of the temples, from the wars of Joshua at Jericho to the battle of Masada, which may have become the model for the battle of the Warsaw Ghetto, which now itself reminds the Jews that they need arms and soldiers and modern technology and cannot rely on the kindness of strangers to prolong or sustain their lives.

And so it is that this sensitivity, this Holocaust memory, has been adopted by the enemies of Israel and used to mock and debilitate. The cry of "Zionism is racism" is an attempt by the Arab countries and their sympathizers to undo the moral right of the Jews to their land, to take away from Jews the justification of history for their new nation. If Zionists are no better than Nazis, if in fact Zionists are Nazis with interchangeable Zs and Ns, both unjustly oppressing a minority who live within its borders, then the basis of granting the new state its legality is eroded away and all the world can join together in taking back this gift of guilt, if guilt is no longer necessary, because the Jews have demonstrated that they are not victims but brutes, like the other brutes that have stalked the globe.

Dr. Mortimor Ostow, professor of pastoral psychiatry at the Jewish Theological Seminary, has said, in an essay based on an ongoing interdisciplinary study, entitled, *Jewish Response to Crisis,* "Thus human sacrifice means not that one gives up something of one's own, but that one murders another and hopes thereby to obtain some religious advantage. . . . By virtue of a sacrifice offered by, or victimizing any member of the group, the entire group feels entitled to special favor. The Hebrew word is zekhut (merit). We acquire zekhut by virtue of sacrifices of others, especially our predecessors." The credit that the Jews won in their own eyes and in the eyes of the world, the thing that is due them because of their suffering, the moral claim they have on God and man, has been redeemed in the creation of the State of Israel. If the Holocaust never existed and there was no sacrifice, then the Jews have no credit. If the Jews behave as badly to others as others have behaved toward them, then the ledger, the moral balance sheet won through such painful sacrifice, is balanced out. This is the religious drama behind the political one today.

Zionism is nationalism and of that there is no doubt, but in theory, in the official view, at least, it simply cannot become racism because by definition Jews are not a race. They are a people believing in Judaism or anyone born of a Jewish mother, or anyone converting to Judaism. They are a group of people self-identified. This is a muddy subject and Jews themselves are in some intellectual logical difficulty when they try to avoid calling themselves a race. Certainly the Nazis thought of them as one. Certainly one can be Jewish without being religious, and certainly this matter of race makes everyone very uneasy. Once it was used to persecute Jews, now it is used to taunt them, to deride their normal nationalistic ambitions.

Unlike the United States of America, the State of Israel at its birth did not intend to be racist. In the Declaration of the Establishment of the State of Israel, it says: "The State of Israel will foster the development of the country for the benefit of all its inhabitants; it will be based on freedom, justice and peace as envisaged by the prophets of Israel; it will endure complete equality of social and political rights to all its inhabitants irrespective of religion, race or sex; it will guarantee freedom of religion, conscience, language, education and culture; it will safeguard the Holy Places of all religions."

The ideal did not entirely become the real. In the occupied West Bank and Gaza the civil rights laws don't apply. Because of the threat to Israel's safety posed by Arab countries, Arabs within Israel do not serve in the army. Their opportunities to succeed in Israeli society are limited by a variety of human prejudices and natural fears that arise out of the continued quarrel over the land. In the day-to-day encounters between the people of Israel and the Arabs who live within the borders of Israel, certain kinds of discrimination, lack of equal educational opportunity, become, while not necessarily sanctioned by the state, embedded in the life of the country. The wars of '67 and '73, the continued acts of terrorism, have fanned hatreds that easily become confused with racism. The unsettled war has intensified tribalism and made it harder and harder yet for both sides to imagine the justifications, the sorrows of the other. The fact is that life in Israel for the Arab is probably affected by race in ways similar to the black in America today, and in the West Bank the laws that apply are not so harsh as the ones we used against Japanese-Americans during World War II. However, the truth is that in Israel, in this new nation, there are two peoples, one a majority, the other a minority, one in power, the other without. Superiority and inferiority are not an official part of the program. The Israeli army has up until recently taught all its soldiers not to hate Arabs because they will be neighbors for the millennium to come. They have tried to avoid racist positions, but the long pull of the quarrel, the continued claim over the same land, have eroded the honorable intentions and the human proclivity to hate has asserted itself. This situation is a setup for calamity, but if we must have nations, then we must have calamities. If we must have nations, then we have the evils that go under the name of racism, the separating out of peoples for reasons of birth: at least so far, at least in this eye blink of cosmic time we call history.

The Holocaust with its Nazi symbols and words is then used by the enemies of Israel in a brilliant political, strategic move to take away the Jewish claim to moral superiority, to claim the sympathy of the world for its dead. The United Nations passed Resolution 3379 linking Zionism with racism on November 10, 1975. The night of November 10, 1938, was Kristallnacht, and the irony of the coincidental dates increased the fear and anger in the Jewish world. Here was History and its dark shadow waltzing together over Jewish graves. This accusation fills the Jewish heart with boundless rage. That Jews have never murdered any mass groups, that even the massacres of Shabra and Shatilla in Lebanon were executed by Christians not Jews, that even if Jewish approval or permission were granted, this does not equate Jewish actions on the West Bank, Gaza, in Jerusalem, in Lebanon with Hitler's wholesale destruction of Jewish life. His Final Solution has no real echo in Israeli politics. Jordanians turned machine guns on Palestinian rioters. Syria murdered 20,000 of its own citizens who were of differing religious positions. Japan has maltreated its Koreans. The French make racist noises about the Arabs of North Africa who have emigrated to their shores. Only for the Israelis has racism become an issue in a territorial war.

Sadly enough racist feeling does have the faintest of reprises in the words of Meir Kahane and those Jews on the religious and nationalistic Right who would simply exile the Arabs, make a greater Israel, Arab-free, and take whatever land and property was left behind. Perhaps in the occupation of the West Bank there does come a kind of double standard of law and justice, of right and wrong, that makes it possible to abuse the civil rights of the Arabs and to punish families for political activity of children. We have seen terrible pictures of Jewish boys beating Arab boys, of Jewish soldiers pulling at Arab women.

Jews have tended to feel that the media worldwide have exploited these pictures, have made them too prominent, have deliberately, in an anti-Israel move, presented the Israelis as cruel occupiers in order to threaten the State of Israel. It seems more likely that the media function under their own inherent limits, looking for instant pictures, unable to explain history or motive or surrounding issues. It also seems likely that the world is relishing these pictures because it relieves the burden of those terrible pictures of the camps. It releases the Gentile world from feelings of obligation to Jews who were victims. Jews who are oppressors wipe out the past guilt. No wonder the world watches each time an Israeli soldier puts his arm out to block the camera view. No wonder these pictures are placed on the front page. It is not simple anti-Semitism; it is not simple pro-Arab sensibility: it is more that the entitlement that the Jews had won through their suffering in the Holocaust, the credit they earned, has now been finished and the world is relieved. Jews no longer victims, no longer have a moral club to wield over anyone else. Now they are wielding real clubs like everyone else. The Arab propagandists understand this situation very well. They play with the Holocaust when they try to send a boat of deported refugees, complete with press and celebrities, to Haifa. They are saying loudly: see the Jews don't deserve the land. They are not innocent sufferers but cruel conquerors. Politically it is a brilliant move. It teases Jews with the image of themselves as British colonialists, as Nazi brutes. The Arabs may have lost on the battlefield but in this game of public humiliation they have managed with great skill.

There are, however, crucial differences between Nazi Germany and modern-day Israel, and for sanity's sake we need to hold on to them. No Jewish spokesman in prewar Berlin ever announced that the Jews intended to drive the Germans into the sea: a statement at the core of the PLO covenant. The Jews believed they were an integral part of the nations whose passports they held, whose war decorations they cherished, whose language they spoke, whose music they played. The Arabs on the other hand believe that they are a conquered people, dealt with unjustly, entitled to the land of the State of Israel, entitled to a country of their own. The hostility between the Jew and the Arab is at least mutual and the subject of contention is a physical reality not a virulent hallucination.

The fight of the Nazis against the Jewish virus was one-sided: it was without a real enemy. Its cause was truly racism not territory, and so today's echoes are not equivalences, and the analogy is so inexact as to be useless, except as political propaganda, except to relieve the world of its moral guilt. It is a particular piece of black humor that Jews should be called racist in a world in which all the European imperialist powers imposed burdens of race on the areas under their domain. Considering the amount of real racism still raging across the African continent, still apparent in France and Germany and England, to accuse the Jews of racist crimes (the Jews who have suffered such devastation because of assumptions of racial inferiority) must make the angels weep or laugh or whatever it is that angels do when human reason fails. Almost all of the 800,000 Jews who lived in Arab lands prior to 1948 have been sent into exile; many have come to Israel. They suffered persecution in

Iraq, Iran, and Syria. They have had their property confiscated and been excluded from education, and their lives threatened. National liberation movements and fundamentalist religious movements in the Moslem world have combined to instigate a holy war against Israel and against the Jews who lived in Arab countries. Neither party to the war in the Middle East, none of the branches of Islam, none of the differing Arab groups, is innocent of racism.

The Zionist dream, dreamed as it was by some of the sweetest, most humanitarian of sleepers, was always nationalistic, and nationalism—a bureaucratic, emotionally laden form of the more poetic expression, a Chosen People—has always had its dark underbelly. Americans know this. We know what we did to the Sioux and the Navaho and the Seneca Indians, the blacks of Africa. We know what we did to the Mexicans and we know what we did to the Vietnamese in the name of national interest. States are by definition difficult places to enjoy variety, to perfect brotherhood. The state by its nature seeks to homogenize, to increase its power, to demolish whatever is in its way. Every state is a Chosen People with an army, with a police force, with a CIA or an Israeli Mossad, that finds ways around laws passed by the squeamish idealist who, while they want a state that offers safety and power, have agreed that there are limits to what they may do to secure their vision.

A small group within the religious Right, the nationalist forces in Israel have gained in power and numerical strength in recent years. They do such ugly things as march in the streets calling "Death to the Arabs." A small band has beaten up Arabs and destroyed Arab stores, smashing windows. They are not supported by the majority of Israelis but they do represent a frightening extreme that has learned from the Holocaust only some techniques of intimidation.

They have little tolerance for matters of democratic procedure and will organize against the constitution and bill of rights now readied by lawyers at Tel Aviv University. Orthodox Jewish religion itself, like all religions, does not have a democratic structure or a democratic commitment at its base. The rabbinical assemblies of ancient times did take a democratic vote on positions and God Himself is said to have bowed to the majority of his rabbis on at least one occasion, but the form of the religion, its willingness to exclude women, the power it gave first its priests and then its rabbis and always its God, is not egalitarian or organized by democratic processes. The Orthodox and certainly ultra-orthodox Jewish religion is authoritarian. The Middle East does not have a democratic tradition. All over the globe there are many more authoritarian governments than democratic ones. Some of those countries that today have elected parliaments and permit free speech will turn tomorrow back into dictatorships of the Right or the Left. Democracy is very difficult for human beings to maintain. Deeply religious and traditional peoples create ideologues who know the truth, have little patience or respect for those who differ. Traditional religion may offer a moral and spiritual path but it is often an obstruction on the road to democratic existence. In this, Israel is no exception, except that, as always, the affairs of Jews take on special heat, glow against the globe as if they are sending messages, as if the Jews were the tea leaves by which the rest of humanity could read its fate. The anger of the Jew against the Arab is not a clear echo of the anger of the German against the Jew, but the resonance increases as a people once despised try on the role of occupier, a role that cannot help but taste sweet after so many centuries endured as the victim.

Racism is a very imprecise word to describe the enmity

of two groups struggling for the same orchard, but no one has yet conceived of a situation in which there might be two chosen people, or three best beloveds, or four carriers of the truth. Fascism, a government that does not protect the rights of all citizens, a government that holds power through fear and is accountable to no one, has a bad name in today's world because of the Holocaust. Hitler may well have died in the bunker, but no one has yet driven a stake through the heart of the Fascist impulse. It surges everywhere: in Reagan's basement cabinet's attempt to bypass Congress, in Chile's treatment of political prisoners, in Soviet mental hospitals, in South Africa's censorship and apartheid rules, and there are some who would bring it to Israel if others do not block them.

The Holocaust, then, pulls internal Israeli politics in opposing directions. On the one hand the memory of the death camps evokes in Jews a particular sensitivity to minorities and reinforces respect for human life, increasing the value of each human being, requiring absolute protection for the minority, and creating an identification with the stranger, even when the stranger is the implacable Arab enemy and not oneself. This, of course, is a universalist view that is as self-serving as it is moral. In practical terms it means that Arab civil rights within the borders of Israel are important and must be considered despite the play of the terrorist's hand. It means that the West Bank and Gaza are liabilities, producing not a greater Israel but an Israel reduced to an occupier, a master with a rebellious and dangerous slave in its midst. It means that annexing the West Bank, building settlements near Arab homes and Arab roads, makes Israel take on the face of its old enemy, forcing women and children to cower as its young men ride by with their tanks and guns.

On the other hand the Holocaust leaves Jews with a memory of what happened to them when they had no state and they had no guns and there was no one to protect their homes and save their lives from the murderous intentions of others. After eighteen centuries of life without power, Jews have come to a moment of apparent power. The turnaround is both exhilarating and hard to believe. The determination to be a strong military power is not only a response to realistic Middle East conditions, to threats by Yasir Arafat and others to drive them into the sea, but it is also a commandment that rose naturally from the ashes of the camps, a commandment that shouts its message so loud that it is hard to hear the call of peace among the moderates on both sides, it drowns out the other voice of the Holocaust which calls for identification with the unlanded, the unprotected, the aliens in the village whose ways are different and whose God has left them without resource to counter your will.

Other traces of the Holocaust are found in the ever chaotic Israeli political scene. Anger with the enemy runs high not just because he is this enemy but because of what the last Jewish enemy had done. Anger in the Jewish mind grows cumulatively from anger with Haman, to anger with Syrian and Roman conquerors, to anger with Spanish Inquisitors, to anger with cossaks and czars and Austrian Grafs until we reach Hitler and Goebbels and Eichmann and Mengele, and the weight of the anger we bear causes us to stumble and to brim over with hate, and who can we hate but the Arab who stands now in the way of our power, our national expansion, our well-earned, long-delayed, deserved gratification.

We can also hate ourselves. We can turn against Jews who are less religiously observant than we are, or against those who are more religiously observant than we are. We can turn against Jews who have been converted by the wrong rabbi or against Jews who have come from abroad or who are darker-skinned or lighter-skinned than we are. The hate that is the result of centuries of anger, anger particularly stoked by the Holocaust, spills into Israeli society and makes it so raucous, so complicated, so unharmonious.

The recent Demjanjuk trial in Israel, which drew huge crowds and endless newspaper and magazine coverage, illustrates that even now the Holocaust holds Israel's attention. It has not been put to rest. It has not become history like the invasion of Titus and wars of Antiochus. It remains as an emotional source of political decision making, as an open wound that festers into the dialogue of the Knesset and weighs on the souls of fourteen-year-olds as well as their elders.

We cannot simply declare the Holocaust a morbid subject and remove it therefore from our souls. We cannot undo the trauma of the six million simply by emphasizing the military victories, the army of reservists, strategists, tank men, radar units, the factories on the Dead Sea, the orange groves and fig trees, the tomatoes growing plump under the plastic bags that cover the drip irrigation, or the role of Israelis in the world markets, intellectual, agricultural, technological. Israel is a country that lives under two shadows. One is the Arab presence that claims the land that once was Palestine, and the other is the Holocaust that makes claims in the name of the dead, that makes it hard to be trusting, to be inventive, to be generous when all the grains of sand in the Negev, in Sinai, do not begin to measure the national bitterness, the personal fear that travels with more consistency than Elijah to every house in the nation.

The Holocaust proved Zionists right. It ended the discussion. The Holocaust has provided a spiritual negative for Israel. They must not, or they dishonor the dead, become the oppressor, the cruel power that bases its actions against people on matters of religion or nationality. On the other hand the Holocaust has made Jews conscious of their vulnerability. It has filled them with rage, it has made some of them feel entitled to any action that serves their need, as if all the moral laws of behavior toward others were suspended because of the Holocaust: as if inverting Rabbi Hillel's famous injunction, they now feel entitled to do unto others what was done unto them.

Although essential, it is not enough, to remember the Holocaust and record its dead and its deeds, but we need, Arab, Jew, Israeli, American, all of us, to look at the Holocaust and see if we cannot elaborate its message, beyond never again, what else is there, encoded in the facts of Final Solution, to guide us?

There may be a healing possible if the Jews and the Arabs can see themselves in the Holocaust mirror. If we can find a nationalism that at least partially satisfies both brothers. Israel needs to struggle with the moral contradictions in a Jewish state that wants to be a democracy, an anti-Fascist, antitotalitarian model of human life. Israel and Israelis are as Herzl envisioned, a normal state made up of normal human beings and as such they are tempted, as are all peoples, to abuse power, to hate the stranger, to allow violence and cruelty to replace law. If the Jews can find a way toward peace, even with the difficulties of Arab hostility, then perhaps they will have become the people chosen to show the way toward a benign nationalism.

Theologian Martin Buber wrote: "We considered it a fundamental point that in this case two vital claims oppose each other, two claims of a different nature and a different origin which cannot objectively be pitted against one another and between which no objective decision can be made as to which is just, which unjust. We considered, and still consider, it our duty to understand, to honor the claim which is opposed to ours, and to endeavor to reconcile both claims. We could not and cannot renounce the Jewish claim: something even higher than the life of our people is bound up with this land, namely, its work, its divine mission. But we have been and still are convinced that it must be possible to find some compromise between this claim and the other, for we love this land and we believe in its future; since such love and such faith are surely present on the other side as well, a union in the common service of the land must be within the range of possibility. Where there is faith and love, a solution may be found even to what appears to be a tragic opposition."

If this impossible tangle resolves peacefully then the entire globe can take heart, can take hope, can look forward to a future without nuclear destruction, without endless human wars. Perhaps the Arab-Jewish conflict is a kind of dreadful paradigm, a test for us all. Can there be nations that live peacefully side by side, can ancient quarrels subside, can the tendency to cling to one's own and despise the stranger be put aside? Martin Buber thought so. In Judaism the vision exists. Jews may have the chance to do something as remarkable as their original conception of one God.

True enough, when Israelis look for someone to talk with, they find they are talking to themselves. Moderate Arabs have been murdered and the Palestinian position shows no central leadership that would move toward acceptance of Israel in the Mideast. There are factions in Israel that welcome this state of affairs because negotiation means compromise and this they do not wish to do. The wind of the Holocaust is at their back. The task is to leap over the impasse, not to welcome it as a means of maintaining the status quo, a status quo that will not be maintained at any rate. The price paid in Israel when the army tries to hide its actions from the camera, when people demonstrate against army policy in the West Bank, when some Israeli boys are refusing to serve in the territories is morally high and moral worth is a good bit of the Jewish capital. The creative political mind, the willing imaginative mind, can find its way. The genius that codified ethics, that designed a partnership between God and man, that struggled with angels on ladders, can now, once again tested, cross this desert too. If not, Hitler has another victory. If not, we may see the fourth disaster for the Jewish people and surely there will come a time when the Jewish spirit will splinter under the burden of the cumulative tragedies.

Jewish-American Politics

DANCING IN THE DARK

Jewish-American politics has been vastly altered by the Holocaust. After the fact, the ineffectiveness of Stephen Wise and the rest of the leadership seems like betrayal. The Bermuda Conference decision in 1943 to do nothing to rescue the Jews except to win the war was not disputed loudly or clearly enough. The not unrealistic fear of anti-Semitism in this country at that time, the assumption that a chameleon-like blending into the American mass was necessary for Jewish progress and comfort, the age-old sense of Jewish helplessness, the attempt to be American and to benefit from the advantages, political and economic, that the country could offer if Jews were less aggressively Jewish—all contributed to an overall Jewish political silence even as the facts of the Final Solution crossed the Atlantic, as rumor, as suspicion, and at last as undeniable reality.

The aftershock brought on a numbing, a disbelief, a sense of shame, of humiliation, of loss, of rage so terrible that it could not be expressed, of fear that it could happen again, of practical concern for the survivors. Gradually, after many years, Americans began listening to the survivors, and Jews determined to preserve the history of European Jewry, to create a record of what had happened, to build monuments and museums to commemorate the dead. Along with the deepening conception of the Holocaust grew a forceful, politically organized Jewish community. This in turn produced an outspoken Israeli lobby, known as one of the most powerful pressure groups on Capitol Hill. It has thousands of members and produces a strong Jewish vote on the well-being of the State of Israel. Groups have formed to organize on behalf of Soviet Jewry as well as other Jewish interests, such as school prayer, support of religious schools, and opposition to quota systems. The major Jewish organizations today meet with senators, congressmen, Cabinet members regularly. They have access to newspaper and television coverage and their opinions and approval are sought by candidates and crusaders of all sorts. The Jewish community would never again sit back and let Jewish interests be set aside for "American" ones. The December 1987 march on Washington in support of Soviet Jews, which drew 200,000 people into the streets, would have been unthinkable in 1941 and occurred precisely because of its earlier absence.

Directly following the Second World War there was a time of self-blame. Why had not enough been done? There was a time to blame the victims: why had the Jewish councils in the Nazi-organized ghettos cooperated so well? There was a time to blame the entire corpse of Jewish Europe: why had they not taken guns and killed the guards? Why had they answered the deportation calls? Why had they allowed themselves to be slaughtered like animals? There was outspoken anger with God and theological questioning. Then there was a time of anger with those who asked those questions. The public furor at Hannah Arendt who raised these issues ended the debate. It became unacceptable to question the action of the victims.

The Holocaust has moved to the core of American Jewish identity. Some say it has too large a place in the American Jewish mind, others say it can never loom too large. The Simon Wiesenthal Center for Holocaust Studies in California can raise hundreds of thousands of dollars on direct-mail appeals for chasing Nazi war criminals, for developing means to keep the memory of the Holocaust alive, and for teaching programs. We are now in a time of setting up memorials, working on presidential and municipal committees on the Holocaust. Long after the trees planted in Israel in 1948 by a still-grieving but still-celebrating Jewish world have grown to maturity, the mail brings new requests for money for memorials, new statues, wings of museums, buildings, and schools dedicated to the victims.

Some members of the Jewish community swung to the Right. Their numbers are small; however they are outspoken and articulate and they have a significant constituency among the Jewish intellectuals. They have not had a substantial impact on the wider Jewish community despite the fact that they have taken center stage, but they have made everyone question old alliances and allegiances. They do not speak for all Jews but they speak a great deal and have made the liberal, universalist, humanitarian Jew duck as the national pendulum appears to be swinging to the Right.

In the late 1970s we began to see more Jewish intellectuals finding in Communism the evil, the source of the infectious disease that could end the world. They began to identify their Jewish interests with the interests of the business community of the United States. This move to the Right coincided with the Soviet stepped-up anti-Zionist campaign, and its 1967 break with Israel, along with the invention of the Zionism-is-racism libel. The tragedy of Soviet Jews who wished to emigrate to Israel and were denied visas surfaced and increased in intensity as refuseniks were jailed, hospitalized for punitive medical treatment, and exiled to the interior. This made Russia the archenemy of the Jewish purpose and thereby made Jews the staunch supporters of the most outspoken anti-Soviets within the American political spectrum. They found in the Communism of the Soviet Union and the variety of Communisms that appeared in the poorer countries of the world the same dreadful, awesome, powerful, dangerous absolute single demon that in Nazi Germany had formerly been found in the Jewish physiognomy, in the Jewish writings, in the Jewish soul.

This anti-Communism, a relatively new thread in Jewish life, owes its existence to a combination of factors. First, the desire not to be a victim anymore, and who were the victims, but the poor, the blacks, the uneducated, and the peasants in South America and the elderly in Miami: secondly, there was among the intellectuals a real disillusionment with the Communist or leftist promise. The Communists in the purges of 1950 had shown that the Comintern could be as anti-Semitic as any czar: that Jewish life was cheap under the Soviet system and that Jewish immigration to Israel would be forbidden as a modern form of imprisoning Jews, of stripping them of their rights, of treating them as undesirables and denying their communal existence. The Rosenbergs may have died as victims of this country's anti-Communist hysteria, but they also died as Jewish fools, because their ideology, the means they chose to become universal human beings rather than vulnerable Jews, would in the end have singled them out as Jews and encouraged an anti-Semitic populace to forget their graves. Totalitarianism, whether Fascist or Communist, cannot allow the diversity, the idosyncratic path, the individualism, that Jews require in order to survive as minorities within a larger culture. This certainty fueled the anti-Communism of the American Jewish Right.

After the Six-Day War the Russians broke off relations with Israel, sided clearly with the Arabs on all Israeli issues, and voted against Israel in the United Nations as often as possible. The Communists in Russia gave Jews the world over every reason to despise them. The Free Soviet Jewry campaign has alerted the entire Jewish community to the implacable enemy of Jewish choice that is and remains at this writing, the USSR.

But some of the Jews who turned to the Right were spurred by more than just anti-Russian feeling. Some of this anti-Communism was inspired by the desire to ride to safety on the backs of the powerful, the rich, the corporations, the old-moneyed interests, the CIA, white Middle America. A group of Jewish intellectuals, some of whom had themselves flirted with Communism in their youth, now looked for safety, for security and protection for the Jews, and where best to find it but in the superpatriots, wrapped tightly in the American flag, in the American comforts of nostalgia and white Christian power. This veering to the Right is a Holocaust response because at its root lies a desire to protect the community, by folding it into the state, by making it a valued yes-man, by identifying its interests with those of the people with money and power and above all, armaments. A people engaged in an anti-Communist crusade will not have the time or interest to turn against Jews. They will support a strong Israel as a domino in their theory of defense against Soviet spheres of influence. In fact such traditional enemies of pluralism, of tolerance, of separation of church and state, as Fundamentalist Christians applaud with the neoconservative Jews the anti-Communist passion plays on whatever stage they are performed.

This Jewish turn to the Right is a Holocaust response because at bottom, when all the rationalizing and the intellectualizing are done, in the tea leaves can be read a wish to shed the victim status and pose, with missile and nuclear submarine, as part of the mighty forces of the West, the invincible forces of "Good." Jews with an army, an Israeli army and an American army on their side, cannot be shoveled off the globe again. The emphasis on arms and warheads of the Right appeals to Jewish vulnerability, appeals to the militarism of those who had been defeated and who vowed never again to be a captive nation. It appeals too to Jewish need to be identified, not only with the brave little State of Israel but with its giant protector who like Luke Skywalker will win in the end over the evil forces of Darth Vader. The problem is that the Jewish view negates other Jewish values and traditional Jewish positions. The identification with the hungry, the discriminated against, the less secure, the excluded, which has been a traditional part of Jewish-American liberal thinking, must be overlooked if Jews are to belong to the apparatus of power.

Some Jews have always been Republican, but the vast majority knew that they were not particularly welcome since social anti-Semitism was fierce in Republican corporate circles. It was clear to everyone, including Jews, that in the prewar days, Jews were not welcome in the clubs of the white Christian Protestant Establishment. They were outsiders and had to make their fortunes in connection with other outsiders. This has changed. The current ebbing of open social anti-Semitism is also in part a response to the Holocaust which made apparent to all people the moral consequences of this particular prejudice, and for a period of time at least pushed anti-Semitism to the fringes of society. It is rumored that Yale University, which in prewar days kept its Jewish quota under 2 percent, now has about 40 percent Jews in each entering class.

Identifying with the power base in the government is a reprise of an old historical Jewish maneuver in Europe, where in most principalities, feudal states, kingdoms, and fiefdoms, the Jews, through exemption from the usury laws, through high literacy and intellectual gifts, managed to serve the rulers in some financial capacity so that they were protected by edict from the anti-Semitism of the populace and given a special role in the functioning of the state. This strategy won several generations of safety. It made many Jews well off, if not wealthy, but in the long run this service to the powers that be ended in disaster as the people, according to Hannah Arendt, inevitably turned against the Jews as their first move in turning against their governments. Currying favor with power did not in the end save the Jews, neither, of course, did identifying with the masses, which tells us that we had best find moral Jewish principles on which to base our alliances, because the fields of the Left and the fields of the Right are equally mined. The cloak of humanism has a hole in its pocket and through it the Jews are dropped. But becoming court Jews only won a temporary reprieve, a possibility of wealth for a few and the same precarious existence for all.

The new Jewish Right is not only following historical tradition, but it is also providing for its members a safety valve that releases anger and goes some distance toward satisfying the unfulfilled need for revenge that has been part of the communal dynamic since the Holocaust. The Jews on the Right do, along with most other Jews and Americans of all kinds, feel a genuine hatred for the Communists. They can also feel superior to the poor, the blacks, and the Hispanics in this country. They can say to themselves, we are the overclass, not the dirty and disheveled, despised ones. They are the victims. We are the elect. For these Jews supplying the weight on the Far Right end of the political scales, there appears to be an understandable unconscious pleasure in this. People have a strong need to be on top, to be socially accepted, to be politically accepted, to be at the place in the society where one can look down with pity or scorn, depending on personal temperament, on others. In human society part of the reward of making it is distinguishing yourself from those who have not. It is not a surprise that Jews who have been so traumatized, so victimized, would in some ways release their anger on other vulnerable peoples. The real surprise is that so many Jews have remained in the mainstream liberal Jewish position and have subdued their rage, continued to hold principles of compassion for others and have consistently turned their national trauma into empathy for others.

At a meeting of Jewish writers and artists during the 1984 Reagan campaign, a debate was held between supporters of Mondale and supporters of Reagan. A young man in his late twenties, in a pin-striped suit and a very thin tie of steel blue, stood up and said, "My parents and grandparents voted for Roosevelt and for Democrats because they thought Roosevelt was Moses and the Democrats would lead the Jews to safety. I am a part of a new generation and now we have power, and now we don't have to identify with the ragged and the poor anymore, and we are the power base and our real interests lie with Reagan not with the party that would tolerate Jesse Jackson, not with the party that keeps muttering about the hungry. We need a strong military to protect Israel. We shouldn't worry about anybody else. When do they worry about us? We need a strong Wall Street to keep our money safe. We are not poor immigrants anymore and we should stop voting like poor immigrants." He sat down to thundering applause.

A small minority of Jews are willing to take their vote and run to the side of anyone who appears to be friendly to their interests. So the strange bedfellows of Jew and Fundamentalist. This friendship is based on the stated affection of the Christian Right for the State of Israel. It is based on solid votes against arms sales to Arabs that have been influenced by Christian spokespeople with political power in the U.S. House and the Senate. It is also based on a misunderstanding of the real attitudes the Christian Right has toward pluralism in this country. The matters of school prayer, public religious displays, freedom of thought in school libraries, all reveal a Christian Fundamentalist position that in the long run cannot maintain an alliance with Jews whom some regard as subjects for conversion when the wars of Gog and Magog are over and the Messiah has returned. Jews who believe this is a real friendship have not understood that religious ideology, the conviction of absolute right on moral and theological matters, cannot result in the kind of live-and-let-live pluralism that has made it possible for the Jewish community in America to become so strong. That Christian Fundamentalists despise and fear Communists because they are atheist does not mean that one day, the right day, they will not also despise and fear Jews because they are Jews. The alliance is one of convenience and could so quickly become a misalliance.

But the Jewish Right in exploring this odd friendship is responding to the lesson of the Holocaust. The people of the host country must be wooed and won. It was disastrous to have the Polish peasant thinking that the Jews were all rich and fleecing their land. It was not helpful to have the French believe that Jews were internationalists who were traitors to the cause of France. The Jews of the American Right have been searching for solid alliances, hoping to make friends among people who appeared to have some power, some influence. If those friends are the most Christian of Christians, well, then, the protection should be that much better. If the truest believers in Jesus are friends of the Jews, then Jews who know what other Christians in other places have done can rest easier in their American beds. The Holocaust has convinced Jews to search for safe and strong friends in their host country.

Host country?: well, yes, even after many centuries, even after the German Jews thought they were Germans, even after the French Jews collected medals in battles for France, even after the Italian Jews had served in government and universities for five hundred years, the Diaspora remained a suspicious lump on the skin of Western civilization. It would be foolish for us now to think of America as anything more than a host country. A papyrus was found on which a Jew in Alexandria in the first century was writing to the tax collector asking for a rebate. He identifies himself as a citizen of Alexandria. Someone else crossed out his identification and replaced it with the information that the writer was a Jew who lived in Alexandria. So old is this illusion of Jewish belonging and so fickle have been the countries that have been the object of patriotism, that common sense tells Jews to expect someone at some point to identify them as strangers who live in the midst. America has a plurality of groups. America has a Constitution and a Bill of Rights and a built-in dream of brotherhood. But ideals can be eroded. Anti-Semitism still runs through this country like spills of gasoline waiting for a match to ignite them. We saw it in the farm country when the banks began to foreclose on the land. We hear it in black circles. We hear it in private conversations and in jokes and we hear it in the acceptance of the phrase Zionism is racism. Protections are only as good as the will of the people and people can will the Japanese into internment camps, the blacks onto the back of the bus and out of the voting places. We know too many stories of German-Jewish men whose war medals were tossed in the ovens along with the bodies of their owners. We should be grateful to our hosts but not expect that their hospitality has changed into kinship.

The problem of dual loyalty is a very sensitive one. It is of utmost importance that Americans do not perceive Jews as being a special interest group that would sell out America for Israel in a time of conflict. All over the ancient world, under Roman rule, Jews lived and traded in a thousand communities and they always sent money back to Jerusalem. Money for the temple, money for the priests, money for the homeland. This problem of dual loyalty cannot be swept under some rug. It exists and is not just an anti-Semitic canard. The Hadassah book and author luncheon in Washington, D. C., in December 1987 opened with eight hundred American women singing the "Hatikvah" followed by "The Star-Spangled Banner." The accusation has considerable reality. American Jews want to be thought of as connected to Israel the same way that the Irish are concerned with the doings in Belfast and the Italians are concerned with the pope and the Armenians still demonstrate against the Turks, and Cubans are concerned with deposing Castro and sing songs of old Havana. But the fact is that Jews alone among all these groups believe that if they don't keep vigilant, if they don't protect themselves, they can be once again stripped of citizenship and ripped from the state. Dual loyalty for the Jewish community is not so much an option but a kind of emotional condition, an ancient binding of Jew to Jew that has always exposed the Jew to the accusation of being an internationalist. The literal truth was that German Jews fought against the French and the French Jews fought against the Germans and likely as not they killed each other. Jews have never turned against a state in which they have made their home and joined with other Jews in some conspiracy. But the truth is also that Jews do have a deep connection to each other around the globe and to the State of Israel. This is a tricky matter. Jews are enriched by the dual connections, the dual traditions, the dual histories. Jews can be patriotic and loyal to two countries and two peoples, just as parents can love two children, just as children can love and need two parents. Divorce would indeed be a nightmare. But if we must ask are Jews loyal to America or to Israel then the answer is ambiguous. Different Jews will fall on different sides of that issue. We are Americans, but, and we don't understand all the nuances of that "but," all the implications for ourselves and our children, or other Americans. We know the "but" is there.

Jews have a special need for the State of Israel, a need that the Holocaust has underlined. This need has caused some Jews to make strange compromises with traditional ethical positions. They have found themselves encouraging the division of East and West in order to protect and secure Israel. They have an understandable need to be this time among the hunters rather than the hunted.

Now if we admit this matter of the profundity of the connection to Israel on the part of the American Jewish community, we must also see that the political divisions and struggles in Israel will all have their echoes here in the American Jewish community. For a while it was considered a kind of treason, an unthinkable matter, for the American Jew to voice objections to the actions of the government of Israel. Give money but don't join the argument. Under all circumstances defend the official position as if the millions of American Jews were all employed by the public relations office of the State of Israel.

From the American point of view this cannot be. American Jews need to know that the democracy of Israel applies to them as well, and that in the vital matters of peace and occupation they can express opinions, talk with one another openly, talk with Israelis. In Israel, opinion is divided on many crucial issues. The government point of view is not the only pro-Israel position. The final decision on all political matters belongs to Israeli citizens, but the special nature of the connection entitles American Jews to pull for this path or that. American Jews are a part of the debate the same way that Israelis are connected, involved with the whole of world Jewry. Open, free discussion will not make us appear disordered, will not give comfort to our enemies. It will simply show democracy, always noisy, never easy or polite, at work.

The unusual nature of the Law of Return, which allows any Jewish person, anyone born of a Jewish mother, to become a citizen of Israel on request, explains the tie between Jews in the Diaspora and those in Israel. The need for that law was written in the death camps. The continued dual-loyalty issue, the overheated militarism of the Jewish Right, in Israel and in America, began with the Final Solution.

The Holocaust has made Jews especially sensitive to and empathetic with what is derisively called special interest groups. The majority of Jews will continue to identify with and vote with the less privileged and more endangered in this country. The moral response to the Holocaust, to increase individual worth and right, will surely continue to be the dominant if not the entire Jewish response.

In the hands of American Jewish interest lies a bargaining chip that cannot be played all the way. One useful only as a bluff. Some American Jews are hoping that the U.S. government will make missile agreements and general détente dependent on the release of Soviet Jews. The pressure to adopt this linkage has already made human rights an issue on the nuclear table. This use of the Soviet Jewry issue along with other human rights matters appears to be a politically skillful tactic, but what if the scenario works in a demonic way? What if the talks break down because of the Russian resistance to Jewish emigration, and several months later there is an increase in political tension, an invasion here or there, or a nuclear accident as Star Wars misfires in our skies or in some way the nuclear holocaust, the death of life as we know it, is brought about, and there is no going back to the moment when the last talks broke off, and the Jewish issue was left unresolved, the lump in the Soviet throat? Could it be that Jewish destiny is to be the tragic figure whose interests end all human interests, including their own? Can we possibly make nuclear disarmament or the last chance for human life free of nuclear terror dependent on our freedom? This is a worst case scenario, but having lived through the Holocaust we can imagine worst cases all too well. It is beyond irony for Jews to place themselves as the obstacles to disarmament. In doing so they could become the trigger that starts the chain of events that lead to the destruction of the world. It cannot be that Jews were chosen for that.

The hawkish positions of the Jewish Right, which include such a deep suspicion of the Soviets that disarmament agreements even complete with verification become undesirable in their eyes, are a kind of madness, the madness of a group that has turned away from trust, from imaginative diplomacy, and puts all its faith in might and force. The Holocaust taught Jews just how important force is, just what happens when you are disarmed, but it should also have taught them what happens when you stop imagining the lives of the people who are affected by your politics. The burnings begin when one group is willing to go to any extreme to further its ideology.

Jews have had a voice in American politics quite far beyond their actual 2 percent of the population. This is partially because Jewish professionals have become part of every national debate and because Jews have voted as a bloc. In its absorption with Jewish safety, the Jewish Right has somewhat diminished the significance of the Jewish vote, which in the long run can hardly be good for Jewish interests, proving only that untempered self-interest can backfire. Holocaust memory attracts Jews to a strong military stance and at the same time it prompts sympathy, empathy for those in this country and others who are disenfranchised from the ordinary decencies of life. Like Dr. Doolittle's pushmi-pullyu two-headed llama beast, the American Jewish community has unresolved difficulties.

Time

THE GREAT HEALER?

In the early years of the Second World War, Winston Churchill said on the BBC, "When the hour of liberation strikes Europe, as strike it will, it will also be the hour of retribution." But not for the Jews. The war trials convicted only nineteen prominent Nazis. It sentenced to death Hermann Goering, chief of the Luftwaffe, Hans Frank, the governor of occupied Poland, Ernst Kaltenbrunner, chief of the SS Central Office for Reich Security, Julius Streicher, the editor of the anti-Semitic *Stürmer,* and eight others, including in absentia, Martin Bormann, chief of Hitler's party chancellery. The trials were dramatic and received world attention, but it was obvious that a handful of men could not have murdered six million. The scales of justice broke under the weight of the dead.

The American intelligence units helped many others to escape. The Vatican provided a passageway to South America for friends of the Church and the vast majority of underlings who stood by, who cooperated, who approved and staffed the extermination camps went home to their families, and continued their lives, suffering only from a limited amnesia that served well to expunge the smell of burning bodies and the sight of starving children. On February 4, 1987, *The New York Times* reported in its obituary column that Gerhard Klopfer, SS general, who had attended the meeting with fifteen top Nazis on January 20,

1942, at Wannsee to plan the mechanics of the Final Solution, died at the age of eighty-one. From 1956 on he had practiced law in Neu Ulm, Bavaria: so short was the hour of retribution.

The Nazi hunting by Simon Wiesenthal and others produced the sensational, informational trial of Adolf Eichmann, but now it seems to recover in its net only old men whose faces may or may not match the pictures on identification cards, with yellowed edges, who have lived for forty years with their wives and children in suburbs of cities like Boston and New York, watching the Yankees and the Red Sox win and lose season after season. The actual Nazi who did the acts of infamy, who picked up babies and smashed their heads against the wall, who rounded up old women and shot them naked besides the trenches, he has gotten away. He is no longer there, in his prime, in his uniform, in his element. We can only punish shadows and exile men with white beards and advanced heart conditions, men who protest their innocence no matter what they may have done and whose families must believe their stories. We can continue to track down others but the majority will be found like Mengele in a grave, identified only by dental records. They will have gotten away with it. Even if we had caught Mengele and a thousand others and even if the world helped us send them to jails, return them to countries of origin, where they could be tried and convicted, that would not satisfy. Our psychological need for revenge, our normal human need for revenge, can never be satisfied. It is vast and deep and runs through the Jewish soul like a flood-filled river that never finds the sea. The Right in the United States, showing perhaps its not so latent anti-Semitism, has spokesmen like former Reagan staff member Pat Buchanan asking why the Justice Department did not go after organized crime instead of running down seventy-year-old camp guards. Anthony Lewis in *The New York Times* answered him by saying that what those camp guards did must never be forgotten. While Lewis has a point most of us would agree with, the seventy-year-olds have achieved oblivion. The world does not share the Jewish passion for justice on this issue and it hardly affects the roil of anger in the Jewish soul to seize these aged, pathetic examples of retribution gone awry. We do squeeze some satisfaction out of the final imprisonment of those who are exposed but this satisfaction is contaminated by our fury at all their years of comfort and continuance, years their victims forever missed.

The threat of punishment by political leaders in the West never did stop the Nazi killing machine. Richard Lichtheim, head of the Jewish Agency in Geneva during the war, wrote to his New York office, on September 3, 1942: "Announcements lately made that the perpetrators would be punished after the war have of course no effect." This is quite the point. The mass murder of a helpless civilian population is a crime on such a scale that we can never deliver punishment or take our revenge. It outweighs our human capacity to judge or be judged. We have no system of law that could punish the German people for standing behind Hitler. We have no way of punishing the Austrians who stood cheering and saluting as Hitler's troops moved into Vienna. We cannot punish a people for a failure to behave heroically. We cannot punish the ones who took over the abandoned Jewish apartments or who turned in stray children who were hidden in other people's barns or basements. After everything, the Jewish nation has to admit an additional defeat. Justice is not possible. The crime was such that the word crime no longer applies. There can be no punishment. If there were it would not be a punishment but a repetition of the original act.

A survivor of the Kovno ghetto, Dr. Zalman Grinberg, wrote in the last hours of the war: "Hitler has lost every battle on every front except the battle against defenseless and unarmed men, women and children. He won the war against the Jews of Europe. He carried out this war with the help of the German nation. However, we do not want revenge. If we took vengeance it would mean we would fall into the depths of ethics and morals the German nation has been in these past ten years. We are not able to slaughter women and children. We are not able to burn millions of people. We are not able to starve hundreds of thousands."

This is true except for the part about not wanting revenge. We want it because we are human beings, but our other moral imperatives, our knowledge of what that revenge would mean, makes it impossible. We would not take revenge even if it were possible. Elie Wiesel has written a novel, *The Fifth Son,* whose hero, son of a survivor, demonstrates clearly that revenge, although devoutly wished, becomes impossible for men who have not turned into barbarians. But that does not mean that the anger that precedes vengeance has left us. The fantasy of revenge, even the occasional act of successful rebellion, sustained Jewish life in the camps and out. Emmanuel Ringelblum, historian, collector of the Days of Sabbath papers in the Warsaw Ghetto, wrote in his diary on hearing of a successful attack on the SS in France, "After the Cologne affair, I walked around in a good mood, feeling that, even if I should perish at their hands my death was prepaid." But we read these words with a sigh. His death was not really prepaid and the deaths of all the others were never paid at all, and the idea of a life for a life is already a debasement of human hope, a success of the Nazi, who had bestialized as well as conquered.

Jewish texts have been clear in their call for revenge on other occasions. "Remember what Amalek did to you on your journey, after you left Egypt . . . you shall blot out the memory of Amalek from under the heaven. Do not forget." Deuteronomy 25:17, 19. The Psalmist had uttered the fiercest battle cry of all: "He will execute judgement upon the nations and fill the world with corpses. He will shatter the enemies head over the wide earth." Deuteronomy 20:16: "You shall save alive nothing that breathes." 1 Samuel 15:3: "Do not spare them, but kill both man and woman and suckling." Numbers 31:17–18: "Now therefore kill every male among the little ones and kill every woman who has known man by lying with him but the young girls who have not known man by lying with him keep alive for yourselves." After the bloodshed of the Crusades, after the deaths of the entire Jewish population of Mainz in the year 1096, each Passover, as the door for Elijah was opened, the leader of the Seder added a call for revenge.

These quotes are not meant to represent the Jewish people as a bloody, vengeful nation. For each of these we could find a balancing quote from the rabbis or in the Scripture which has to do with forgiveness of the enemy, understanding of the other, respect for the opponent, respect for life. The theme of vengeance is there, however, and it is there because of a strong, natural human need to be avenged when one has been wronged. Our need in these days is no less than it was in biblical times. We are, when it comes to the Holocaust, without resource, without belief in God's actions on our behalf, without the conviction that Elijah himself will come down from the heavens and roll the heads of the indifferent nations. We are in fact left with some guilt over the knot of hate that forms when our need for vengeance solidifies. Our anger is hard to live with because we believe it wrong, not civilized, not proper. Most of us push away this wish for vengeance, deny it to ourselves, deny it to our children. We may go as far as boycotting German products for a generation or so but even that we see does not affect the Wirtschaftswunder and in real terms gives no satisfaction. Revenge on such a scale cannot be effected except perhaps by God, and the God of Jewish history has shown far more interest in punishing Jewish transgression in the last two thousand years than in vanquishing enemies. So we are left with the collective pain of the Jewish people unassuaged, denied by some, forgotten by others, and festering inside us, no matter how many memorials we build and how many museums we create and how many tons of relevant archives we collect, or how many stories we make, art or journalism. Nothing eases as vengeance might, if vengeance were possible: but it is not.

So one of the impossible Jewish tasks is to absorb the anger that arises from this unmet need for revenge, to absorb it in such a way that we do not turn it on ourselves or on other innocent peoples or indulge ourselves in collective rages that might hurt the body politic. Was the invasion of Lebanon perhaps such a moment where we not only said never again, but allowed our military to move forward to crush the enemy, to take revenge for the rockets that had been fired a year earlier at settlements in the north, to use the military to express the communal need for killing someone in our turn? Did Shabra and Shatilla happen because Israeli military personnel pretended to themselves that they were good Germans watching the trains go by? Are the Jewish boys who face the rioting teenagers in Gaza thinking of the Warsaw Ghetto where the Jews were themselves an occupied people? Did they perhaps think of themselves as French police watching the departure of Jewish children from the Gare St. Michel in the center of Paris? Were they playing the bystander who does not interfere in a masquerade of misplaced revenge? It seems possible. The world screamed at Israel, Holocaust, Holocaust; they yelled because they wanted to believe that the Jews were no different from anyone else. The moral superiority of the Jewish people sticks in the world's craw, tasting of guilt and shame, marking the great civilizations of the West as moral midgets, as Goliaths more beast than man. How happy they were at the pictures of bodies lined up against the walls of Shabra and Shatilla: perhaps David too was an ethical dwarf? The world could not understand the anger that Jews bring to all current events, the singeing of all things in the flame of Auschwitz. How could the world possibly understand Sharon's men playing the role of the Christian mayors and the Christian councilmen of Prague and Warsaw, of Lublin and Vilna?

Chaim Herzog, president of Israel, said while visiting Bergen-Belsen where 50,000 people died, "I do not bring forgiveness with me nor forgetfulness. The only ones who can forgive are the dead: the living have no right to forget. The mourning of your deaths will be kept in eternal memory in our hearts—not to sustain an enduring enmity, not to maintain a sterile and debilitating hatred but to gain strength and steadfastness." This statement strikes us all as moral and correct, dignified and proper. The only problem is how does one prevent enduring enmity? How does one admit hatred but prevent it from sterilizing the future?

How can the Holocaust be turned into knowledge for the next generations? Surely reality lags behind rhetoric: far behind.

There is the tale told by Rabbi Abraham Joshua Heschel about the train from Warsaw to Brisk on which some young businessmen in high spirits found themselves in a car with a small bearded fellow with a simple cap on his head and a sacred book in his lap. They asked the man to join in their card game and passed him the bottle from which they were drinking. When he refused, they threw his cap out the window and pushed him out of their compartment.

When the train arrived at Brisk, a great crowd was in the station. They surged forward to the car and with many salutations and blessings greeted the famous Reb Chaim of Brisk. The rabbi was not only a renowned scholar but a holy man whose compassion was legendary. The young businessmen got off the train and chased after the rabbi. "Please, sir," said one, "forgive us, we didn't know who you were." "I cannot forgive you," said the rabbi, and the crowd was stunned by the rabbi's uncharitable words. "I am the Reb Chaim from Brisk—you did nothing to offend me. You must ask forgiveness of the little man in the car with you, the one who had no name."

This story explains our bind. We cannot forgive for the dead; on the other hand we can't help being angry for them either. Because we are a part of them, they are a part of us, just as the old man on the train both was and was not the famous rabbi from Minsk.

This anger, of course, feeds into our entire history of Jewish suffering. Many Jewish intellectual leaders have deplored the so-called lachrymose Jewish history which emphasizes Jewish suffering at the expense of the richness and joy, the ethical and traditional vibrancy of Jewish life. While one would like to think of Jewish life in the most positive ways possible, nevertheless the long story of slavery, exile, inquisition, exile, pogrom, that lead to the death camps makes it hard to separate out the cultural achievements from the disasters that surrounded and often prompted them. The Jewish holidays themselves, from Purim to Pesach, have incorporated the nation's peril and the nation's disasters. As Yerushalmi said in his book, *Zakhor,* "In the Middle Ages only that which was transfigured ritually and liturgically was endowed with a real chance for survival and permanence." So the murders at Blois and Mainz were turned into prayers that could and did apply to similar events in the past and future. It is not possible to pull apart the Jewish historical experience with all the tears that accompany it from Jewish ritual, traditional, and scholarly life. We can emphasize other parts of Jewish existence, we can, as the Israelis do, place flowers and fruit symbolizing renewal, on the graves on Remembrance Day, but we cannot banish the lachrymose themes without altering the body of Judaism. Hawthorne's story of the bride with the beauty mark on her face who dies when her husband attempts to remove her blemish is a good warning for us.

But this history is hard to live with: we don't know how to carry so much pain. We don't know how much longer the wealth of the tradition can sustain the weight of historical experience. Hirsh David Namberg, angry at the continual Jewish grief, wrote in his diary after the pogroms of 1903: "We Jews are fated is another kind of glorification—like dogs we lick away at our own blood. We collect and collect and collect bloody tears and sorrows." In the ghetto of Vilna, a young man, Abba Kovner, planning to run to the forests and organize a partisan resistance to the Nazis, spoke to an older man, Zelig Kalmanovitsch, a leader in the Jewish community. The man advised him: "Against evil of such magnitude one cannot go with force. Our strength is our powerlessness. We are fated to be like all of Abraham's children." He meant that like Isaac on the altar we had no choice but to wait for rescue, for the Covenant to be fulfilled. The young man, Abba Kovner, disagreed and went off into the woods and took up arms and survived the war, but he remembered the old man's comment and preserved it for us.

The British rabbis recently held a conference in which they said that the Holocaust was not a unique event in Jewish life but simply another in the line of disasters. Some of the scholars present linked the Shoah to the destruction of the First Temple. One rabbi insisted that the Holocaust be placed into the religious framework: the people were bad and God has spoken to them harshly. Many of the ultra-Orthodox communities in Israel and in America have taken this view. They believe that the people who were murdered by the Nazis had somehow become impure and that the Nazis were no more than God's avenging hand. This position solves certain theological problems that the Holocaust has presented and if accepted it enables the Jewish religion to go on unchanged. But of course most Jews will not find acceptable a position that explains the Final Solution in terms of Jewish wrongdoing. The nature and whereabouts of God's protective hand are not so clear, and the uniqueness of the Holocaust, its continuing traumatic effect on the nation, cannot be wished away.

The akedah, the offering of Isaac by his father to his God, brings us to the peculiar mixture of sacrifice and blood that seems to accompany chosenness. The Christians describe a God who sacrificed His son so that man could live in eternity. Why did He have to do this? Why could God not simply revoke His punishment of Adam after he had eaten from the forbidden apple and relieve the angels with their burning swords of their duty at the gates of Eden? The answer seems to lie somewhere in our psychological makeup, somewhere in our need to design sacrificing fathers, sons who die but don't exactly, burnt offerings that are meant to be stand-ins for human sacrifice but sometimes become the real thing. This bloody theme of father and son, of smoke and fire, keeps being recast in different molds. It is a theme that has stirred our collective imagination and there is no reason to believe that we have yet seen its final form.

If Jews have borne more than their share of suffering because they believed they were given a special gift, a Torah, an ethical and spiritual way of life that could lead the world in times of darkness, then today with no certain end to the human story in sight, they may feel ready to let someone else play the part of Isaac on Mount Moriah. They may be tired of licking wounds; licking wounds can become a habit, an illness even. They may be ready to cast aside the position of moral virtue, of moral value that was implicit in the idea of chosenness. The rabbis have said often that the concept of the Chosen People does not imply superiority to others, only special mission, special service. But no matter how often that is repeated, the idea of chosenness holds at its kernel an undeniable sense of worth, of favored status, of special value in a spinning cosmos. If one is going to be a light unto the nations, then one must shine brighter, stand on higher ground, than the others, and this conviction will not help in the popularity contest that nations sometimes call war, sometimes define as an autoimmune response. We must admit that the claim to chosenness, no matter how it is soft-pedaled, no matter how it is presented, cannot win friends or place the Jewish people inside a magic circle of safety.

But without it, the sacred essence, the secret core, the covenant, is abandoned and with its loss goes the sustaining purpose of Jewish life, to wander on toward a destiny that holds a key to the puzzle of human life, a key that will prove itself indispensable someday. This is our political, psychological, religious quandary.

Pearl Goffman, a survivor, now of New York City, said when Jews in Istanbul were murdered at prayer in their synagogue, "You can't say it will never happen again, because it does. Why? Because we are the Chosen People, chosen for what?" In the light of the Holocaust, Jews must find a way to define chosenness, so that it does not bring a bitter smile to the lips. They must find a way to be chosen without provoking the resentments of others. This is a task for theologians, for politicians, for the nation as a whole. It is a task made harder by the Holocaust which has left the Jewish spirit more isolated, more depressed, less flexible, less comfortable in the larger world, than ever before. The Holocaust has affected Jewish self-esteem. To be so devastated, so decimated, so powerless in the face of death is to lose self-esteem. Dr. Mortimer Ostow, professor of pastoral psychiatry at the Jewish Theological Seminary of America, has said, "The challenges to Jewish self-esteem have characterized even tranquil intervals in the many centuries of exile. The very word tolerance implies a difference in status between the host community and the Jewish guests. I should like to suggest that the assault on Jewish self-esteem by external tolerance or intolerance had played a shaping role in the determination of the character and personality of the individual Jew as well as the behavior of the Jewish community and the culture it has created.

Specifically, I believe that we can attribute, to some extent, to the need to overcome Jewish low self-esteem: Jewish ambition and success, Jewish cohesiveness and divisiveness, Jewish loyalty and disloyalty, Jewish self-effacement and Jewish ostentation." When our sense of self is wounded we grow more angry and distressed, and these now intensified feelings are a part of all Jewish existence today. This pain makes it more difficult for us to reconcile with the other nations of the globe in a human circle that has neither a head nor a foot, a better or worse, a more loved or a least loved. They have the mark of Cain on their foreheads. We are the better-loved Abel: the favored Abel bleeding in the fields. Everyone wants to be Abel. Everyone is furious if he or she is labeled Cain. No one wants to be the victim. Yet everyone wants to be good, the way the victim is good. Martial Israel changes the matter slightly, but it is too early to see how much and for how long. The entire matter of tribe against tribe, of brother against brother, is just as it was in the beginning, in the first pages of Genesis—philosophically, logically, theologically, psychologically; no one has imagined a way out.

The Holocaust was the culmination of anti-Semitism. As Hannah Arendt said, "The subterranean stream of western history has finally come to the surface and usurped the dignity of our tradition." She means the tradition of Western culture, of Goethe, and Mozart and Michelangelo. Certainly there is no reason to be surprised that within a generation of technical possibility the camps were in place. At the time of the Panama Canal scandal in France, the newspapers printed editorials calling for the "Jews to be stewed in oil or pierced to death with needles. They should be circumcised up to the neck. A new gun should be tried out on the 100,000 Jews in the country." Some two decades later the esteemed writer Celine said, "Jews have caused all European wars since 843." He demanded the massacre of all Jews. That anti-Semitism is endemic to Europe is as true as the fact that the cathedrals of France are glorious and the flowers along the Danube bloom in the spring. That human beings have always shown the need to sacrifice with blood to increase their tribal health means that the Holocaust may be both a Jewish tragedy and a human proclivity, something natural in the beast that we cannot repress, any more than we can stop ourselves from evacuating or eating. Robert J. Lifton, professor of psychiatry and psychology at John Jay college and the Graduate Center of the City University of New York, says, "Anti-Semitism may be a perverse quest for the immortality of one's own group in which we encounter the impulse toward mass murder in the name of more life." It may be that one group really needs to sacrifice another, weaker group in order to assert its vitality, its power. This process may have nothing inherently to do with Jews or how they picture themselves, or what tales they tell their children. Since history has shown us that the tribes get larger and more inclusive and the bloodshed extends as well, we may be heading toward a time when humanity sacrifices itself and the drama ends. We can now begin to look at the Holocaust as both a specific Jewish tragedy and a human event. We do not have to count the nationalities or religions of the dead to hold both facts in mind without contradiction. Styron rushed to universalize. Jews have held to the particular. Both views are necessary and correct. Richard Rubenstein in his book *The Cunning of History* said: "Nevertheless for all its uniqueness, the Holocaust must be seen against the horizon of the unprecedented magnitude of violence in the twentieth century. No century in human history can match the twentieth in the sheer number of human beings slaughtered as a direct consequence of the political activity of the great states. One estimate of the humanly inflicted deaths of the twentieth century places the total at about one hundred million. As fewer men have fallen prey to such natural ills as the plague and epidemic, the technology of human violence has taken up much of the slack. Those who nature did not kill before their time were often slain by their fellowmen."

It seems likely that anti-Semitism was simply the disguise mass murder wore in the years 1941–1945. Since then we have seen it on a smaller scale in Cambodia, and no doubt even without Jews as its object it could happen again, in another time to another people. That Jews feel and remember the Holocaust with particular pain testifies partially to the limited capacity of all human beings to imagine ourselves as members of another group. We still have deep tribal loyalties which blind us to the humanity of others. Those anthropologists who are finding connections between human social behavior and our biological programs that enabled us to survive as a species might conceive of our tribal fierceness as a biological defect, like the predisposition to cancer or Alzheimer's disease. It may be a defect linked to some other strength, like our capacity to care for our young and build our families. It may be that just as we can never grow wings out of our shoulder blades but could invent airplanes, we can find some artificial way around our natural limitations. Religion, like the early designs of the Wright brothers, seems to take us not quite far enough.

Hannah Arendt writing of the banality of evil was searching for the explanation of how the technology and the ideology merged into an effective killing machine. She did observe for us the peculiarities and dangers of mass culture and their civil services. Her explorations do make clear how it was possible that a murderous plan of such proportions could have been put into place and executed. Claude Lanzmann in his film *Shoah* illustrates her thesis, by running the railroad trains before our eyes over and over again, producing a kind of numbness, a kind of contradiction with the landscape that finally became less noticeable, as the hours of the film passed. He filmed the ways in which the technocracy turned murderous without full individual consciousness and participation. In this view of the Holocaust modern society permits a moral cloud to numb its response and proceeds to follow orders, to follow plans, to devise ways of accomplishing ends that are more efficient and cost-effective than others and in so doing permits horror to occur beyond the control of the individual will and outside the sight of the moral regulators that most of us carry within. This theory of the Holocaust, while it does add to our understanding, remains only partial, exposing for our study only half the tale.

All the accounts of the Holocaust are filled with personal anecdotes of violence and sadism. Here a child is ripped apart, here a pregnant woman is raped and stabbed in the abdomen. Here an old man is made to scrub the streets with a toothbrush, there a guard gives bread to his dog

in front of a starving child. The Holocaust is not only, as one looks closely and listens to the stories of the survivors, an impersonal event, a technological mistake, a result of the trains running on time in response to orders given by zombies, people whose moral cores had gone to sleep, but also, perhaps even foremost, a collection of acts of sadism committed by men and women given permission by the larger culture to tear limbs, to strip the dead, to shoot babies suckling at their mothers' breasts. This eruption of individual sadistic behavior needs examination. What are we, the human animal, that we did this? What is the core of this behavior? While the end of the world will come about because of the technocracy, because of evil that has been institutionalized and permeated with paranoia and depersonalized beyond our reach, the path toward that moment will be paved by individuals who can push babies into gas vans and cover the still living with dirt. In December 1987, former national security advisers Henry Kissinger and Zbigniew Brzezinski were asked on television for their opinions of the current INF treaty. Both men were very glum and their worried faces appeared in our living rooms like two prophets of doom. No they were not happy. The treaty might give someone the idea that nuclear weaponry with its capacity to kill every living thing on this globe was not essential. They felt it was technically impossible now to do without nuclear weapons. They had good technical reasons for wanting the weaponry in place. As they spoke, our living rooms were filled with echoes of the Gestapo leaders Lanzmann had interviewed. Today's statesmen were also involved in a problem that did not have a human face. They did not think of burned flesh and charred fields. They thought of delivery systems and on-site inspections. They were saddened at the loss of some of their missiles. Here the sadism of the individual human act, the burning of children and the destruction of life, has once again been buried in the language of the technocrats. How did this happen? How does the individual capacity for cruelty become transformed into Henry Kissinger counting warheads? We need to understand this connection if we are to save ourselves next time. We need most desperately to think of the Holocaust not as a political event alone but as a psychological upheaval, one in which we are ourselves revealed. We need to find the courage to examine the face of the Holocaust as it appears in every man, woman, and child on this globe.

If Jews can find a way to assert the uniquely Jewish calamity of the Holocaust while still tying the event into the course of human history, we may help avert the next and probably final disaster. If we continue to make the rest of the peoples of the world feel uncomfortable if they refer to the Holocaust, if they mourn their dead or ask us to mourn their dead: the Poles, the French, the Gypsies, the homosexuals, the Cambodians, the Hindus, the Moslems, then we intensify the world's sense of Jews as accusers, as victims, as morally superior, as set apart, as marked. The Holocaust belongs to the Jews, because of the numbers of Jewish dead, because of the nature of the intended genocide, because only Jews lost their communities entirely, their men and women and children. Only Jewish houses of worship burned and only Jews were stigmatized by repressive laws and isolated in ghettos. Only Jews were rounded up and shot in trenches and gassed in vans. But if we do not let this fact subside into the larger fact that man did this to man, that bloodletting is a human invention, akin to a religious device, to give shape to the days, to bind group into history, to make history and meaning out of our confused state, then we will never be prepared to avert the next calamity. Timothy Garton Ash, writing in *The New York Review of Books,* said, "To argue that the Holocaust was unique plainly does not require one to view it in total isolation, far less to assert that there have been no other examples of genocide. If I say this murder is unique I am not saying there are no other murders." Perhaps it is time to study the connection between the murders. Adi Ophir, writing in *Tikkun* magazine, said, "Why is our Holocaust myth so dangerous? Because it blurs the humanness of the Holocaust: because it puts an infinite distance between one type of atrocity and all other types of human atrocities, because it encourages the memory as an excuse for one more nation unifying ritual and not as a tool for historical understanding."

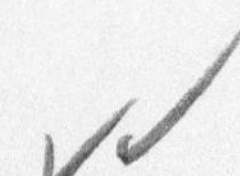

It does not dishonor the Jewish dead to say that the Holocaust was both universal and particular. It does not obliterate the memory of those who died to focus on the Holocaust as a means of understanding the human demon that is all of us.

A forest fire begun by a streak of lightning moves quickly across the mountain range and burns within hours 100,000 acres of formerly green and rich land, leaving black ash where insect, butterfly, and bird once flew among the leaves of maple, ash, beech, among the white birch and dark pine, home to thousands of animals, whose charred bones now decay on the blackened dirt. But ten years later the new shoots of pine have grown to shoulder height. The dead branches have crumbled into the ground and bunchberry and steeplechase are growing along with the wild primroses and the birds are back and the insects are crawling and the deer and the squirrel, the fox and the moose, are roaming again through the forest night. In forty years life has returned no matter how vast the devastation.

We saw pictures of a million Biafran children dying in the sun with swollen bellies and eyes closed with pus: flies crawling over small clenched lips. Twenty-five years later, after the civil war, there is a new generation of babies, round and healthy. Pregnant women walk about in flowered dresses. In the villages memory of the disaster lasts, but there is also music and food, weddings and births. This view is perhaps harsh because we place so much value on individual life, and so we must, so is the way humans experience life. If we do not value each soul we become like the slugs of the sea: species not selves. But the facts of biology are different, are not so concerned with our individual destiny, with our inalienable rights. Nature, the globe we sit on: it goes on and replaces us with the same rapidity with which it reseeds its forests. Nothing can be remembered forever with the same heat as it was first experienced. There is over man and beast a life-force that subsumes our individualities completely. This can be used to justify destruction of human life or it can be simply observed and understood, recognized and used to help us heal, to go on, to let the dead go. We cannot, no matter how hard we try, preserve the names, the faces, the towns. We cannot, no matter how we would wish, bring back to life the murdered.

The Bal Shem, the founder of the Hasidic movement, said that "Forgetting is exile and remembering is redemption." If we forget we dishonor the past and we dishonor the dead. We have no right to forget or to allow others to forget, but on the other hand redemption is not as simple as mere remembering. Redemption will lie in understanding, in examination, in finding a way to remember that allows the reseeding of the forest, that permits the natural energy of life to take over with its enthusiasms and its partial but inevitable callousness to the past.

We will have to understand that the Christian need to forget, to deny, to distort, stems from their inability to face what their culture, their religion, has done. Creating more guilt, engaging in a match of virtue and moral superiority, will not clear the air. We have to understand that behind each outrageous denial of the past, with each attempt to universalize the Holocaust before Jews are ready, lies the pain of facts not yet faced, realities such as that most of the SS men who proded the unfortunate onto the trains went to a Lutheran Sunday school and learned their Christianity there. The combat between those who want to remember and those who insist that we forget will begin to be over when we recognize the motives behind the positions.

Dr. Steven Leul, has written in *Psychoanalytic Reflections on the Holocaust,* "The Holocaust must become less of a painful emotional problem for us and remain predominantly in historical, philosophical and intellectual contexts for our children. . . . But our obligation, unless we choose to remain wedded to masochism, is to promote healing and foster wellness in our young. We must find a via media between the obligation to remember with its unavoidable sadness, the obligation to lessen the obsessive rumination, the corrosive cynicism regarding human possibilities, the distrust of 'the other,' all of which point to damaging links to the Holocaust."

The British Chief Rabbi, Sir Immanuel Jacobovits, said, "Would it not be a catastrophic perversion of the Jewish spirit if brooding over the Holocaust were to become a substantial element in the Jewish purpose, and if the anxiety to prevent another Holocaust were to be relied upon as an essential incentive for Jewish activity?" He called for a shift from "the survival of Jews to the survival of Judaism. For without Judaism, Jewish survival is both questionable and meaningless."

The Jewish nation would do well to finish this absorption with a tragic past. Psychoanalyst Dr. Martin Bergmann has written, "To be traumatized and in mourning inevitably affects a group's ability to assess current threats and deal with them effectively and realistically. Therefore we have to steer a careful line between not forgetting and excessive remembering. Too much stress on remembrance is an oppressive way to live. It is often overlooked that the process of mourning should ultimately lead to some measure of resolution and resignation without despair."

David Biale, director of the Center for Jewish Studies at the Graduate Theological Union in Berkeley, California, wrote, "The Holocaust needs to be divorced from what it tells us about Jewish history and connected instead to the other special dilemmas of contemporary politics. Remembering the Holocaust cannot prevent a recurrence." This means that the unique and Jewish nature of the Holocaust should be gradually understood in the context of human behavior. It means that the prospect of nuclear war, which would be world genocide, must preoccupy our minds and use our monies and intellectual resources.

While Jews are moving toward a universal understanding of the Holocaust, Christians might give this process the time it needs. They cannot bury the Holocaust by historical revisions that make all catastrophes one, Stalin equals Hitler and Caesar equals Pol Pot, before they have come to terms with the anti-Semitism of Christian society. If Christians no longer deny the Jewish essence of the Holocaust tragedy by emphasizing the general evil, their own national dead, by omitting the mention of Jews on their monuments, in their history books, then Jews will not feel the urgency to remind everyone, who is guilty and who is innocent. If Christians are able to examine the flaw in civilization that led to the death of six million human beings, then the guilt, which is only abstractly, only in the vaguest tribal sense, collective, can end. The wound can be cauterized by truth and by honesty and then, only after that, by finally letting it go into the past where it increasingly belongs.

Elie Wiesel says, "The Holocaust is a unique Jewish tragedy with universal meaning." The argument about the universal or particular nature of the event can be resolved by an acceptance of the truth in both positions, an acceptance of the experience as both Jewish and human. There will be no need for us to protect the Holocaust as belonging to Jews when the entire world can recognize that it happened to Jews, and it happened to human beings, and it belongs to our common human history as well as to a particular Jewish history. It seems like an argument over semantics but it is not; in this sometimes painful discussion we see an evolution toward a more complicated sense of ourselves as separate in the stories of our cultures and yet bound together in one fate. This view may keep us on the planet a while longer.

Anger, the anger of the young Jewish woman watching the Russians rape German children, has not yet gone away. It smolders on despite the passage of time, the aging of the guilty, and the hopelessness of revenge. Anger could not be kept out of this book although the book is about healing. All we can do is confront and accept that anger: Jewish rage, Christian anger, black anger, Soviet anger. Unless we let it surface, unless we allow ourselves to see it, we can never put it to rest. The healing process begins with the acknowledgment of anger and the helplessness it engenders.

Collective guilt is as unpleasant an idea as any other group generalization. It makes individuals furious and resentful. It turns them away from the real events of the Holocaust and it makes them unable to examine the degree to which the institutions, the culture to which they belong, are in part responsible. Christians have to resist this guilt and its implications without doing violence to the truth or to the dead. After understanding Jewish anger, after understanding Christian anger, Christians can then universalize the Holocaust, absorb its revelation about human nature, without feeling morally uncomfortable, bitter, because the Jews have made them morally uncomfortable. Then the true work of weaving past into man's story will have begun. Echoing the Bal Shem, either deliberately or because the Judeo-Christian tradition is in fact one river, West German President Richard von Weizsacker said in a speech to the West German Parliament on May 8, 1985, "There can be no reconciliation without remembrance. The experience of millionfold death is part of the very being of every Jew in the world. Seeking to forget makes exile all the longer. The secret of redemption lies in remembrance." True, but not entirely: remembrance must not mean indulging in guilt that is inappropriate. Today's Germany contains a majority of those who could not have participated passively or actively in the Third Reich. Remembrance must mean just what it means to Americans who think of slavery: a pain in the heart, an ache that reveals nationalism as a two-faced friend, one that bears watching. If Christians can come to terms with the Holocaust without forgetting its specific Jewish target, then the bridge we have to cross to get over this divide will be in place. We can go on. The Holocaust can then truly become universalized into a warning of what can happen when man allows the destructive urge, the death instinct, the sadistic pleasure to gain the upper hand. The Holocaust will stop being a Jewish obsession, one the Christian world is constantly trying to ward off, as if to neutralize an evil eye. It will become of use to all peoples in our common effort to stay the nuclear tide, the pollution tide, the bloodshed of religious wars and other threats we have not yet imagined but are sure to appear.

If Jews are not victims, what are they? Will cohesiveness and identity be lost if we should find ourselves in a new place? These are questions that are more challenging than frightening and the answers to what we are and what we are for will be many and splendid.

It is unrealistic to hope for too much and yet how fortunate it would be if Jews now entered a time of renaissance, a time of new creativity in art, in literature, in ethics, philosophy, and politics. We could learn how to be ourselves without denying the rights of others. We could explore matters of chosenness and perhaps find definitions that will amaze. The Arab-Israeli conflict, if it ends in peace, in new alliances, may be the beginning of a new way for humankind where Cain and Abel can share the land and be equally beloved in the eyes of their God. The land of Canaan can be the place where human invention shows itself strong enough to prevent disaster, to circumvent hatred and to begin the solutions to the kinds of terror that have led mankind into war after war, right to the edge of the final destruction. The Jewish nation may have some moral purpose in the scheme of things, a purpose not as victim, not as the sacrifice others offer to their Gods, but to ease the sufferings of all, to develop technologies that can feed the hungry who live in arid places, to develop medicines that will bring men longer and more useful lives. It is possible that the Jewish nation has been selected not as a totem of pain but to add its part to the creative vitality of life. It is time for us to face down the angers of the past and to concentrate on the future. If we just go about our lives, whether or not this brings the Messiah, we will certainly lend variety and breadth to the human endeavor.

If we do not find a way toward what Dr. Robert Lifton has called a species self, one that does not override the particular but is still included in the universal, we will be wrapped in our Torah and we will surely burn and our history end. Elie Wiesel, our first spokesman from the camps, has received the Nobel Peace Prize, and in his speech he said that we must be ready to help all those in need, we must serve as carriers of empathy, as watchpeople for the vulnerable. He has said that, "when he needed help, no one came and therefore he must come when anyone cries." This statement is our renaissance, our perfect Star Wars defense shield. It is our new beginning: green shoots among the ash, maybe.